# The Homestead Haunting

## Of the
## Oley Valley

Jeffrey A. Dengler

Copyright © 2024 by Jeffrey A. Dengler

All Rights Reserved.

No part of this book may be used or reproduced by any means, graphic, electronic, or mechanical, including photocopying, recording, taping, or by any information storage retrieval system without the written permission of the publisher except in the case of brief quotations embodied in critical articles and reviews. No patent liability is assumed with respect to the use of the information contained herein.

Although every precaution has been taken in the preparation of this book, the publisher and author assume no responsibility for errors or omissions. Neither is any liability assumed for damages resulting from the use of the information contained herein.

ISBN 979-8-218-98895-1

Printed in the United States of America

# Dedication

This book is dedicated to Randy, Alice, and Lisa. By sharing your story, you have provided hope and understanding to those who face similar experiences. In honor of your journey and in gratitude for your help in illuminating the path for others, this book is dedicated to you and your entire family.

For more true haunting stories,
please explore my other books,

*The Minersville Mansion*

*The Spirits of Shoemakersville Road*

# Table of Contents

# Introduction

<br>

EVERY PERSON, EVERY family I helped over the years has become a part of me. These experiences, along with my own awakening, have helped me understand, grow, and open my eyes to all that is around each of us. I can look back at these moments in time and know I did my best to help each family understand why they were experiencing the activity in their home. These are my personal feelings. So many friends and family have spent their valuable time and energy over the years. I am grateful for each and everyone that has joined me in helping so many. My wife has been by my side throughout it all. I couldn't have done it without her.

Over the years, one home has bothered me because I never finished what I started in 2010. Why is this? I am not quite sure I can come up with one reason for it.

All the stories I heard made me approach with caution. I say this not for my own well being, but for our children's sake. With hauntings, we always take measures to protect ourselves. Our intention is to not bring anything home with us. The possibility is always there. I didn't want anything with negative intent to wreak havoc in my home and affect my kids. This was a huge concern for me at this moment in time. It was the main reason I didn't continue to seek the answers. I've done my best and will continue to do my best to protect my family and myself from some form of entity, spirit, energy from following us home. That is always my intent, but on occasion, our home gets a visitor. In this instance, I proceeded with caution. After reading this story, you will understand why.

Another reason is just life happens. We become busy with family, work, new cases, new opportunities, etc. The years honestly seem to fly by.

This property is saturated with a long history of unexplained phenomena. Some of the firsthand accounts shared with us are enough to make your skin crawl and chill you to the bone. The homeowners were reluctant for us to dig too deep because they believed negative energies were the cause of the haunting.

One thing's for certain, this property never totally let go of its grip. Did it creep its way into our psyche, or was it still reaching out, reminding us, somewhat toying with us to finish what we started?

Fourteen years have gone by since we first visited this

farm. It is crazy how fast time has passed.

In order to write this story, I have to go by my own memory, as well as everyone's remembrance that was involved in this investigation. Each of us have certain recollections that remain deep in our memory, while other things appear to fade from its grasp. It is truly fascinating how the human brain works. How does it know we forgot something, but can't remember what we forgot? What makes one memory stay while others fade? I can remember a certain occurrence from that time so vividly, and someone who experienced it with me has absolutely no recall of it. Does one's own perception and tolerance to fear somehow affect their ability to remember? Why does the mind block certain events, yet others stand out? All of it intrigues me.

Several attempts were made to reach individuals who had a connection to this property, but I was met with reluctance to discuss the matter.

I made my best effort, but I will always respect everyone's reasoning and privacy.

Since I was a child, I have always questioned everything. I have been told endless times over my life, "You ask a lot of questions." That childlike wonder has never left me.

I keep an open mind. We evolve as we get older. Our perceptions change. I look at things differently than I did in 2010.

I feel confident in my abilities, my growth, and my

trust in both myself and the otherside.

I believe everything happens the way it is supposed to at the time it is supposed to. I feel the time is now to revisit the past and finish what we started.

# Chapter 1

## The Doors Slam

THERE IS A quaint village in eastern Pennsylvania overflowing with history and home to one of the state's earliest settlements. Driving through this area instantly transports you back in time.

Prior to European immigration, the Lenni Lenape People inhabited the area. The name of this town is derived from the Indigenous language and the word "Olink," meaning both hollow and kettle, or "Oolikhanna," which translates to grunting place or place where bears are. Both words are said to come from the Lenni Lenape language. In the early eighteenth century, the Swedes, Swiss, French, English, and Welsh Quakers were prominent in the area. Pennsylvania Germans, also known as the Pennsylvania Dutch, arrived soon after.

As you can imagine, the mixture of this population brought with it a variety of ideas and beliefs.

Ironworks, mills, craftworks, tanneries, gristmills, and farms began to thrive in this region. For the most part, the Lenni Lenape and settlers in Oley lived in peace together. However, as hostilities escalated and the threat of the French and Indian War approached, the Indigenous population began to leave the area.

The immigrants that originally settled became less and less over the coming years, but a considerable amount of German descent remain in what has come to be known as part of Pennsylvania Dutch Country. A lot of these descendants and others who call Oley, Pennsylvania home still see, hear, and sense these early settlers roaming their homes and properties. I feel many residents within these hills and valleys, and, quite possibly, this entire village could be hearing and seeing the echoes of the past. I have visited quite a few haunted properties that are part of this historic area, all with their own spooky tales about things that go bump in the night.

Just outside of Oley, along what is known as Oley Turnpike Road, there are several farms and homes that contribute to the area's rich history. Many Germans settled in this area of the Oley Valley referred to as Snyderville and Limekiln.

One farm on Oley Turnpike Road was experiencing so much paranormal activity it prompted the homeowner to consider an exorcism to rid the home of any evil that potentially lurked within. Why did they feel this way? Was this farm haunted by one of the early settlers? Did someone die tragically at one of the local mills, tanneries, taverns? Was it a previous owner of the property? Since the Lenni Lenape were considered the original keepers of the land, were they still close by protecting it? Did someone living in the home, either knowingly or unknowingly, open doors to the paranormal? Did the current homeowners just perceive it as evil? All these questions would cross my mind over the coming days and years.

This farm was owned by relatives of my good friend, Shawn. His aunt, Alice, and uncle, Randy, owned the property for over forty years.

There are two homes on the property that sit close to the road. A stone driveway separates the two.

The main home was where the owners lived. It is a small single-family home with white siding. There are three cement steps that lead to a wood porch painted red. The porch is supported by four white poles. On the center of the roof is a three-window dormer.

The other dwelling is a red brick farmhouse that was a rental property and is larger than the main house. Looking at it from the front, it does not look to be too big, but viewing it from the side, it is definitely a more sizable structure.

The brick home sets back off the road about the same distance as the main house. It has three wooden steps painted gray. This porch is smaller than the one on the other home. The front door is framed by a roof held up by four white antique-looking columns.

Shawn contacted me originally in 2010 to tell me about a frightening experience he had in the brick farmhouse. I will never forget this story because every time I recall it, it makes me laugh because of what Shawn did to his buddy, Larry. I asked Shawn to retell his account of what happened on that day. This encounter for Shawn opened the door for me to experience this farm for myself.

January 5, 2024, Shawn writes:

This is a true story. One that actually happened to me and my buddy, Larry. It was a few years back in the one home on my aunt and uncle's farm in Oley, Pennsylvania. A little background to this place. I always had a creepy feeling about this farm ever since I was a kid. While nothing ever had happened to me there, I just could not get over the energy I always felt whenever I was there. Not a bad feeling so much, but an unsettling vibe. Like a presence of some kind. An unrested energy. Now there are stories of how this farm is haunted and it's even in a book. However, nothing had me more convinced about this farm being haunted like the experience Larry and myself witnessed. With that said, it was a beautiful day outside this one afternoon. I believe it was early to mid-fall because it was really comfortable temperature wise. Larry and I worked for my father, and were hired by my uncle to do some remodeling work. My father sent us both to the farm to do a job. We were to fix some capping around the outside first floor windows and do some wood trim work in the living room and kitchen. Larry heard some of the stories already that would go on around the farm and said he felt kind of uneasy being inside, so he would go outside and do the windows while I worked inside. Not feeling real easy about it myself being in that empty house alone, I decided to play a prank on Larry. While he was tapping away at some of the nails around the window on the outside of the house, I waited until he bent down to grab some more nails. At that point, when he wasn't looking, I quickly stood in front of the window on the inside of the house so I was face to face with him. I had my eyes wide open with a possessed look on my face, plus

I was doing a shivering motion with my head. I have never seen a 6'4" 240 lb. guy turn pale white like that in my life. He nearly threw the hammer through the window at my face. He was so shaken up, he came inside to tell me what an ass I was for scaring him like that. I was standing there laughing at the situation and just like that, BAM!!!! Simultaneously, both heavy solid wood doors slammed shut on us. Both of our hearts just about stopped. We paused and stared at each other for a minute, wondering what in the hell just happened. We dropped everything and left the house. It was as if whatever was there was upset with me. Like I made a mockery of it or something. Some people said it was probably the wind. In my honest opinion, there is no way! No way at all. Not a single window was open, and both doors of the house were both opened inward. If the wind came in one of the doors, there is no way it would slam the other door closed. Especially with one door facing east and the other door facing south. It doesn't make sense to me. Not to mention the exact timing of the situation IMMEDIATELY after laughing at Larry. NOPE! I'm convinced the place is and always was inhabited by spirits or entities. I remember that experience very vividly because it honestly scared the living shit out of me!

I laughed at this story when it first happened, and I could not help but laugh as I read Shawn's account fourteen years later.

I would never have gone to this house if it were not for Larry and Shawn's chilling experience. I also knew Larry. He is the one that told Shawn's aunt about my work with the paranormal and mentioned to her that maybe I would be willing to investigate her property.

Next, I received a phone call from Shawn asking if I wanted to check out his aunt's haunted farm. He explained to me that his aunt had a local paranormal group investigating prior. She wanted us to come and conduct an investigation to see what we could capture compared to the other team.

Shawn got everything set up, and we agreed on a date to go to this property. We met on the evening of May 21, 2010.

# Chapter 2

## Not Another Night

ON THIS PARTICULAR evening, Shawn met my wife, Tami, and me at the farm. We also brought along Katie, who lived across the street from us. We have known her since she was a child. Katie spent a lot of time with our family going on trips and hanging out at the house. We treated and thought of her as family. Katie invited her good friend, Ann. Also joining us was a friend of mine named Steve, as well as his wife, Lydia.

Steve previously asked me if he could join us on an investigation sometime, so I invited him and his wife to this one. The only other time Steve came with me was when we visited a cemetery right up the road from this farm.

We all met in the lane that separated the two houses on the property. The day was overcast with the high temperature that reached 80 degrees. The sun began to set as we gathered, but the high humidity of the day still lingered. The owner, Alice, came out of her home.

After greeting each other, Alice began to tell us about the property:

> The main home, which my husband and I live in, would be off limits due to the extreme activity that happened in the home. We don't want to stir anything up again. It's been quiet there. It got so bad, I didn't know what to do. I didn't know at one point if I had to go as far as an exorcism.

We completely understood and respected that request.

The farmhouse that was aside the main home was where she wanted us to investigate. They wanted us to talk to the current occupants, Patty and Woody, to hear their claims and help them understand what was happening in their home.

Alice said:

> We are having trouble keeping people in the rental farmhouse due to all the activity. The occupants prior to the current ones were a Spanish family. They became so scared one night that they slept in their car. It was winter and very cold outside, but the family felt safer sleeping in their car than staying in the home. When daylight arrived, they packed their stuff and left. They told us they could not stay in that house another night. When we went into the house, there were crosses and other religious objects hanging everywhere on the walls.

We looked at each other with an expression that said, "What are we getting ourselves into?" Yet, at the same time, we were eager to explore the house.

# Chapter 3

## The Green Room

ALICE WALKED US over to the farmhouse and knocked on the side door. Patty came out to greet us. Afterward, she welcomed us into her home. The side door was the entrance into an enclosed porch. There was a step and then a door which led directly into the kitchen. This room was painted a yellowish-green color. As we walked in, there were older-style white cabinets above a porcelain sink and counter to our right. The sink had the old-fashioned stainless faucet with separate handles for hot and cold water and a soap dish attached to the center of the faucet base. To the right of the sink, a set of floor cabinets ran along the wall to the corner of the room and then turned at a right angle toward the door through which we entered.

A ceiling fan hung overhead. The windows were bare with no shades, blinds, or curtains, which gave the unsettling feeling of being watched.

Patty stopped in the kitchen a few feet from the door.

I asked, "Can you tell us some of the activity that you are experiencing?"

Patty started by telling us a story about what she encountered in the area we were standing in:

> I was walking across the kitchen and heading towards the door to enter the enclosed porch when, all of a sudden, I got pushed very hard and with enough force to knock me over. I ended up on the floor. I didn't slip. I was definitely pushed. I felt the shove, and it terrified me. I'm not the tiniest person, so to knock me off my feet definitely took some force. My boyfriend, Woody, and I hear voices, hear conversations, hear what sounds like a marble roll across the floor, sounds of multiple footsteps walking around including up and down the stairs, but the shove scared me the most. When you go to the top of the stairs to the second floor, there is a bedroom to the right. I will not enter that room because it scares me. I actually have a latch and lock on the door. I unlocked that door just in case you wanted to go in? Straight across at the top of the stairs is our bedroom. I see a figure in that room. One night, I woke up to a figure standing beside the bed. I think that figure came from the attic. I don't like going into the attic. I put salt across the threshold at the door because it scares me.

I said, "I would like to first go in that room with the lock, if that's okay?"

Patty gave me a look of disbelief that I wanted to enter that room.

Patty answered, "Yes, and you are welcome to go anywhere in the home to investigate."

She went outside and sat with Alice and Lisa, Alice's daughter, who also decided to join us for the night.

Woody was in the living room watching television. He was recently diagnosed with cancer and due to his weak state, he would be staying in the living room while we investigated.

Patty stated we could go anywhere in the home, but we stayed away from the living room to give Woody some privacy.

We walked across the kitchen and turned to go upstairs. There was one step then a landing. To the left was the staircase, and straight across the landing was one step that led to the dining room. We made our way onto the landing and continued. Once at the top, we stopped and noticed the latch on the bedroom door to the right. The lock was open as Patty stated, but it remained through the latch. Patty was so frightened by this room; she didn't feel safe removing the lock completely. Seeing her fear, I can only speculate she slid the key in, unlocked it, and went back down the steps as fast as she could. What we all noticed right away was the thick layer of salt poured across the threshold of this door. Patty mentioned she put some at the attic door, but we also noticed it now at this door. Salt has been used for centuries to ward off evil and for protection. Here it was used to keep what they perceived as an evil spirit from crossing the threshold. They wanted whatever they felt was in that room to stay right where it was.

There are those that believe thresholds are a magical space, a bridge between two worlds or dimensions. The phenomenon is known as a liminal space. It is thought spirits can get stuck within them.

Was a spirit or energy form trapped? By placing salt, Patty believed it would protect her from whatever was in that room and prevent it from stepping over the threshold.

We made note of this, looked at each other, and knew we had to be cautious as we entered. Every instinct told me to turn back, but curiosity kept me moving forward. Hesitantly, I turned the knob and opened the door. I did not know what to expect as the door slowly swung open. We each carefully stepped over the salt line and entered the room. It had your typical household items such as a mattress, which was leaning on a dresser, a sofa, a fan, and other things scattered about, and it looked like it was nothing more than a storage room. Even though we heard the claims and witnessed the lock and the salt lying on the floor, the room just felt like any other normal room at that moment. Everything appeared fine, but I knew in my gut, not everything is as it seems. The room was calm and quiet. Whatever frightened Patty so much, was not ready to reveal itself just yet.

As our journey through the upstairs continued, we decided to split up and explore other parts of the house. I set up a video camera at the top of the stairs on a tripod facing down the steps. Several of us went back into the room that Patty kept locked, which is also where she claimed to hear a marble rolling on the floor. We called it the green room because it was painted simply a bright lime green color. Just like most old farmhouses, the windowsills were inset, which made them a perfect seat. No curtains decorated the two windows, only blinds. Among the storage was an old sofa on the opposite side of the room from the windows. Our friend, Steve, sat on the sofa along with Lisa, who decided to come up and join us. The rest of us remained at the windows facing the sofa. With Katie standing to my right, I sat on the windowsill operating the video camera. Ann was standing next to Katie, and Tami was on my left. By this time, dark was setting in, so I started to record using night vision.

Within five minutes, Katie said, "Did you see that?"

I asked her, "Did we see what?"

Katie replied, "I swear I saw a person peek around the corner in the doorway!"

Shocked, I said, "Seriously? Which side of the doorway?"

Katie went over to the door and pointed to the left side of the door frame.

As she pointed to the area, "Right here the head looked in," she responded.

Immediately, I reviewed the footage on my camera. The doorway was just out of frame when Katie saw the figure. This happens a lot during investigations and can be so frustrating.

I continued to record Steve and Lisa on the sofa, but this time, my eyes stayed focused on the doorway in case the figure decided to peek in again.

As Steve sat on the sofa, he held a piece of equipment called a Mel Meter. The Mel Meter measures electromagnetic field, EMF, and the surrounding temperature. It is believed that when a spirit is in the immediate space, the EMF reading will spike. When we first walked in the green room, the Mel Meter reading was between 0.0 and 0.1, and the temperature was 83 degrees. That would be considered the base reading for that room, and if anything fluctuates outside of the base reading, then that would be something to note.

Steve said, "C'mon, you had it at a 1.7, and it dropped down to 80 degrees."

Just as the words left Steve's mouth, I noticed an anomaly through the camera viewfinder. It was coming in from the area of the doorway, moving across the room to my left and in front of the sofa. It glided in a curved path and seemed to go directly into Lisa's neck as she sat on the sofa. In the paranormal field, people use the word orb. I like to call it spirit energy.

The combination of events so far left me completely astonished and mindful of the activity. Whatever was haunting this place was now aware of us and it was making itself known.

# Chapter 4

## Penny for Your Thoughts

TAMI, KATIE, AND Ann decided to go to the back room, which was located at the top of the stairs to the left. It was also directly across the hall from the green room.

Instead of a door, the room had a curtain hanging in the doorway. All three entered through the curtain and found an empty room with paneling on the walls and a hardwood floor. Once inside, they each sat against the wall in different areas of the room. As they settled in the dark, they began to have general conversations between each other. During the discussion, it sounded like something was thrown.

Startled, Tami said, "Did you hear that?"

Both Ann and Katie agreed they heard something hit the floor. As the women continued talking, there it was again, a light, sharp clinking sound. All three turned on their flashlights to see what caused it. None of them saw anything, but they were certain the noise came from an object hitting the floor. They decided to leave the room and find me to let me know what had just happened. As they stood up and began to exit, Tami noticed several pennies on the floor that neither of them noticed prior. She picked up a penny and tossed it. All agreed that the sound matched what they just heard. What was the significance of a penny? Sometimes people refer to finding pennies as messages from spirit or someone who passed on. Was it something that was available and easy to throw, or was the reason more threatening?

Within a short period of time, Katie saw a figure peek around the doorway, I saw an anomaly come in from that direction and travel in a curved path and go into Lisa, and now the three women are hearing what sounded like pennies being thrown, all happening on the second floor.

Steve met up with Lydia downstairs, and they both went to the basement, while Shawn and I decided to go to the attic. Since Patty seemed terrified of both rooms, I wanted to first head to the green room and to the attic next. I took a ball along to the attic to see if a spirit could move it. The attic door was in the bathroom. This was odd as I was never in a home where the attic entrance was in the bathroom.

When Shawn and I reached the attic, it was sweltering. We both agreed we were not spending too much time up there. While standing at the top of the stairs, across the room, I noticed three white chairs sitting between two windows. A fourth chair was sitting on an angle in front of the right window. The creepy scene appeared like something out of a horror movie. Compared to the green room, the attic made me feel extremely uneasy. It was obvious why Patty did not like being in this space.

"Is anyone with us?" Shawn asked.

I questioned the following:
"Who is making themselves known to the family in this house?"
"Do you sit in those chairs and look out the window?"
"Why do you stay here?"
"Can you move the ball I placed in the middle of the floor?"

To avoid having heat exhaustion, Shawn and I kept our questions brief, then decided to return to the second floor.

We headed down the stairs that led to the bathroom. I took the lead with Shawn just behind me. My foot left the last step, and I turned right into the dark bathroom that awaited. As I walked across the floor, my eyes scanned around the room. Since the bedroom light was on, it illuminated the bathroom just enough that I saw Tami standing in the bathtub with the shower curtain only partly open. As our eyes met, she put her index finger up to her mouth to tell me to be quiet. Knowing she was up to something, I kept talking to Shawn to keep him distracted. I passed by Tami and went through the doorway. Just as Shawn walked past the bathtub, Tami reached out from the shadows and grabbed his arm. Shawn let out a high- pitched scream. Tami and I began to laugh so hard we could not breathe. The laughter brought us to literal tears.

Shawn yelled, "Oh my God! That scared the hell out of me!"

There were digital audio recorders present on all levels of the house. After each recorder was reviewed, we could hear Shawn scream at different octaves due to the distance between the recordings from each floor.

We take what we do very seriously, but we always have a little fun in the process.

Shawn and I wanted to go outside to cool off from the heat of the attic, but decided to go into the main bedroom first. While there, Steve and Lydia passed us on their way to the attic.

I asked Steve, "Anything happen in the basement?"

Steve said, "We kept hearing what sounded like drumming. I'm not sure where it was coming from. We are now going to head up to the attic."

"Good luck. It is hot as hell up there," I replied.

Katie and Ann were in the back room, the one that had the curtain for a door.

Upon entering the main bedroom, we captured a male EVP, electronic voice phenomena. As we walked around the room, one specific area made a clicking sound when one of us walked on that part of the hardwood floor. Each time I walked over that spot, I tagged it on the audio. Tagging is simply saying out loud any sounds that are heard while we investigate. This is done so when the footage is reviewed, I do not second guess what the sound may be. When I stepped on the noisy floorboard a second time, I tagged it by saying, "Click on the floor again."

A voice was captured immediately after I said that. It sounded like a male voice saying, "Joshua." We were only in the room for a few minutes. I wanted to try the Radio Shack Hack while we were in the main bedroom. The Shack Hack is a small radio I bought at Radio Shack. For those that do not know what Radio Shack was, it was a store where you could buy electronics, electronic accessories, a few toys and batteries. It went out of business years ago. The small radio I bought there could be taken apart and rewired to scan different frequencies. It became known as the Radio Shack Hack. After rewiring this, instead of one station or frequency heard, it would keep scanning through the frequencies at a fast pace. The idea is as the scanning of the frequencies is happening, the spirit world can communicate using a speaker. This radio has now become what is known as a ghost or spirit box where you tune into certain radio frequencies simultaneously. It allows spirits to utilize the radio waves to form actual words, which we can hear. Various forms of ghost boxes were available over the years. I was on the fence when I first became familiar with this method of communicating with spirits. I have come to trust that it is a valid technique to receive messages from the spirit world. To understand the spirit realm, we must think in terms of energy, frequency, and vibration.

I turned the box on and asked, "Is anyone here in this room?"

A reply was heard. It sounded like a male saying, "No."

Seconds later, another male was heard saying, "Yeah, speaking."

After reaching the attic, Steve and Lydia knew they were not going to stay there too long either due to the extreme heat.

Steve said, "We have four more minutes up here. Please do something. If you want to hang around here for one hundred years, move the ball. Rent's not free."

Immediately after Steve's comment, a voice was captured on the digital audio recorder. We couldn't decipher what was being said. What was very strange about the reply was the voice sounded computer generated. It was not a human tone. Listening to it today, it reminds me of what you would hear using a piece of equipment called the Ovilus.

We heard Steve and others walking in the hall and footsteps going down the stairs.

Steve passed us on the second floor and said, "We are going out for a smoke break."

Shawn and I were the only two that remained upstairs. Everyone else went outside to get air. Shawn saw me looking at the EMF meter.

He asked, "Did it jump?"

I said, "Yeah."

Shawn was referring to the meter spiking. We continued out of the bedroom and down the stairs to meet up with everyone else.

There was a night vision camera placed in the hallway the entire time. As we walked down the steps to meet everyone outside, an EVP was captured on the video recorder's audio track. The voice sounded like it said, "Gene says hi." It could quite possibly have said Jean. Was it referring to a male or female? Did we misinterpret what we heard? These audio captures were only noticed while I reviewed the footage the next day.

After every investigation, I spend several hours, even days, reviewing all the audio and video footage. This can be a very lengthy process depending on how long the investigation takes. If we have, for example, four individual cameras set up and we recorded for four hours, then it would take me sixteen hours to watch the footage.

Now adding individual audio recorders that may be used throughout the home, it would take even more time to review each one. It all depends on what type of investigation we are conducting that would cause the review time to be lengthy. This night, we had individual cameras due to the fact we weren't going to be there long. If it was an overnight investigation, then we would more than likely use multiple cameras connected to a DVR.

It was interesting that we captured audio directly after the meter spiked.

When we capture what we feel is evidence, it is always beneficial to also capture some form of corroborating evidence. This could be in the form of audio, video, photograph, meter fluctuations or spikes, or personal feelings. When we can back up one piece of evidence with another, it holds more weight to not only us, but also to the homeowner.

We went outside and gathered with everyone in the side yard where Alice, Patty, and Lisa were sitting.

I asked Tami to come to the basement with me since we had not gone down there yet. Shawn decided to come with us. We spent about fifteen minutes taking EMF base readings, asking questions, and seeing if we would get any of the meters to light up. Nothing out of the ordinary happened while we were there, besides what sounded like the drumming in the basement, so we decided to go back outside and meet up with everyone.

Our stay only lasted a few hours because we didn't want to take too much of their time since people still lived in this house.

We mingled around the yard and the lane separating the two

houses.

*Katie, Steve, and Lydia on the lane.*

Shawn wanted to show me the well around the back of the house.

Shawn said, "I was always weary of the well out back. Don't know why, but I remember as a kid always hating being around it."

We walked approximately thirty yards behind the farmhouse. The walk back there was dark and eerie.

Shawn said, "This is it, right here under the blackberry bush and the walnut tree."

We stood there looking at this raised area of the yard under the tree. There was a thick 8'x 8' manhole type cover on it.

Standing there sent chills down my spine. Honestly, being outside on the property at night was very unsettling. The best word to describe it was spooky. At any moment, it felt like something would reach out of the darkness and grab one of us. That is a common feeling for most people walking in the dark, but this property heightened that sensation. We asked questions while back there. Nothing was heard or captured on the audio recorder.

We ventured back and met up with everyone in the yard aside of the farmhouse.

I looked at Steve and asked, "What did you think?"

Steve said, "I thought it was cool, but I think Lydia was bored. She was expecting more to happen."

I explained to Steve that it's the way it goes sometimes, and we can't guarantee anything. It was very possible that we did capture audio or visual evidence, but I wouldn't know that until I went over all the footage.

Steve said, "Oh yeah, I get it. It's cool."

I always find it interesting why there can be multiple people at an investigation, but not everyone experiences something. Is it being at the right place at the right time, or does it have to do with the individual themselves? Experiences with paranormal activity are highly subjective and can be influenced by psychological, environmental, and personal factors. Certain people may be more sensitive to subtle changes in their environment. Their heightened perception could make them more prone to noticing things others do not. Another reason could be that some are more open to interactions, and spirits or entities might choose these types to communicate with or even attach themselves to.

It is important to note that the causes of a haunting and the experiences resulting from them are not black and white as many perceive: there are many variables at play.

# Chapter 5

## Truth or Consequences

STEVE AND I started talking about a family graveyard, which was located under a mile from the farmhouse we were currently at. Steve, Tami, Katie, and I visited the cemetery six months prior. During that visit, I photographed a figure standing by the cemetery wall. When we take photos, we always take at least three in a row. That way, we can compare them. If something is in one photo and not in another, then it is significant, and we want to analyze it.

*Figure  captured at cemetery wall.*

This particular cemetery and property have always been of interest to me since I was a child. I urge anyone reading this to research the Schneider Farm and the story of Susanna Cox. Without going into too much detail, beginning at the young age of thirteen, Susanna lived at this farm as an indentured servant. In 1809, she was hanged in Reading's City Park after being accused and convicted of killing her newborn child. City Park was the location of Gallows Hill back in those days. After many years of researching, I have come to the conclusion that the history we are told is not the reality that happened regarding certain events in time. I believe this to be the case regarding Susanna Cox.

As Steve and I spoke, Shawn asked about the place.

I said, "We can still go there tonight if you want?"

Steve added, "Yeah, it's really old. Some of the tombstones date back to the Revolution and are written in German."

I informed Shawn about the figure that was photographed by the cemetery wall during our visit six months ago.

Shawn replied, "I'm game. I'd like to check this out."

Tami and I walked up to Alice, Lisa, and Patty to let them know how nice it was meeting and thanked them for allowing us to investigate the farmhouse. We mentioned that after reviewing all the footage over the coming days, we would definitely be in touch if we captured any evidence. After saying our goodbyes, we headed to our cars.

I had mixed feelings leaving the property. Looking at the brick house as we headed out on the lane, I wished I had more time to investigate. My curiosity urged me to go back inside to search for answers. Did we do enough? Will we be able to validate Alice and Patty's experiences? At the same time, the concern was, will something follow any of us to our next destination or back to one of our homes? A haunting isn't confined to a physical place. It can also linger in your thoughts long after you have left.

We drove further down Oley Turnpike Road, headed for Limekiln Road, and met at what was once the Schneider Farm. As soon as we parked in front of the farmhouse, the current owners came outside. They remembered me from before.

I asked them, "Is it okay if I spend a little time back at the cemetery again? I have a few friends I want to show it to."

They said, "Yeah, that's fine. You can go back. Just be careful since it's dark."

"We will. Thank you. We won't be too long," I said.

Tami and I walked back to our cars to meet the others.

I informed the group, "They said it's fine, we can go back."

Sixty to one hundred yards behind the farmhouse sits the cemetery. To access the cemetery, there is a dirt path between the house and the barn. In the dead of the night, we followed the lane and approached a stone wall surrounding the graveyard. As we entered through the wrought iron gate, I reminded everyone about the random holes in the ground and where the tombstones were broken that we noticed on our last visit. The holes were bothersome for one reason: we could hurt ourselves by accidentally stepping in one, and there could've been some animal living in a hole. Since the tombstones were broken and so old, I figured some people buried there were missing them. Due to age, the tombstones were difficult to read. We shined our flashlights on them at different angles to try and decipher what was written on them. Many were written in German. After looking at them, Steve noticed one name he recognized. The name appeared to be Jacob Geehr. He was one of the men that worked and lived on the farm the same time Susanna lived there. Jacob is the one who allegedly found the dead newborn in the outbuilding wall.

Steve, knowing the history from discussing it with me, walked onto the grave, facing the tombstone. I had my digital audio recorder placed on top of the headstone.

None of us expected what Steve was about to say.

Steve demanded, "Jacob, if you lied about Susanna, raped her or anything, you are a piece of shit and a coward! I hope you burn in hell!"

As Steve said the word hell, he stomped forcefully on Jacob's grave as if his body was beneath his foot so he could teach him a lesson. We all looked at each other in disbelief at Steve's actions. Everyone knows how much I am against provoking any spirit or energy. I always want to conduct ourselves in the most respectful manner when trying to communicate with the other side.

Steve decided to provoke, which could quite possibly come with repercussions. The potential is always there when investigating but provoking something may bring a consequence one may not want. That was a realization within hours of leaving the cemetery.

# Chapter 6

## No Rest for the Wicked

TAMI AND I arrived home. It was like any other night prior to bed. We had a dog named Buster. Tami took him out to do his business, then we headed to bed. Buster was a small dog that didn't take up too much room, so we always permitted him to sleep at the foot of the bed.

I need it as dark as possible in the bedroom so I can get sleep. Tami and I were lying down in complete darkness. Usually, we feel and hear Buster jump at the foot of the bed, walk in a circle, then lie down. We would always hear his collar jingle as he would do his nightly routine, but what we thought would be a normal night of sleep ended up leaving us completely baffled.

As Tami and I lay there, recapping our night, we both heard Buster hit the bed with a heavy thud! Our bed shook.

Buster let out a yelp and ran out the bedroom door.

Startled, Tami and I sat up, confused by what just happened.

Tami said, "What the hell was that?"

I responded, "It literally felt like someone lifted Buster up over their head and body slammed him into the foot of the bed. He even cried out as he ran out of the room!"

Tami said, "Yeah, what the hell?"

We both got up. Tami turned the bedroom light on. Both of us searched for Buster. We found him lying on the sofa.

Tami said, "C'mon buddy, let's go to bed."

Buster froze in terror. He did not want anything to do with returning to our bedroom.

Tami and I, tired and seeing that Buster was not hurt, left him on the sofa and went back to bed and drifted off to sleep.

That sleep didn't last long because close to 3:00 a.m., we were abruptly awakened when our bedroom light came on. The only way to turn our bedroom light on is by the switch, which is located near the bedroom door. Immediately going from a pitch-black room to a bright light really shocks the system. Once again, we both sat up, looked around, trying to focus our eyes and comprehend why our light was on, all while in a slight brain fog from being in a deep sleep just seconds prior.

Tami asked in a concerning tone just above a whisper, "Jeff, why did our light just turn on?"

As I surveyed the room, I said, "I have no idea. What the hell is going on?"

Tami got out of bed to look at the light switch.

"Jeff, the switch is flipped up!" Tami exclaimed. "Who did that?"

I responded, "I have no idea. I thought it was one of the kids at first, but they are in bed and sound asleep."

Concerned, Tami replied, "That doesn't just happen, and I don't like it. First the dog, now this."

I said, "Turn the light off and see what happens. Let's try and get some sleep."

Tami turned the light off, and we ended up getting through the night without another incident. We talked about our encounter on a few occasions the next day and kept replaying it in our heads. None of it made sense. We couldn't logically explain what happened, so we basically accepted the theory that someone followed us home from the Oley farmhouse and/or the cemetery we had gone to afterwards. I was leaning towards the cemetery due to what Steve did. My belief is he upset someone or something. It was angry or wanted to try and frighten us, to tell us to think twice about coming back to Oley. Since we went to two places, I could not identify who was making their presence known.

Our main concern has always been the safety of our children. We always worry about anything following us home and it affects them. My wife and I would try our best not to discuss too much of the paranormal around them, but kids listen to everything even when you think they are not. The dog forcibly thrown in our bed and the light coming on in the middle of the night troubled us because of our kids. Luckily, nothing woke them up or frightened them in any way.

Whatever it was, something decided to pay me a visit a couple of nights later. I was lying on my side facing the side of our bed. Something interrupted my deep sleep, which caused me to open my eyes. It was that feeling you get when someone is staring at you. Within inches of my head was an evil looking face staring right at me. It alarmed me so much I actually swung at it. My fist went right through its snarling face, and it just disappeared as I tried punching it. That was my first instinctive reaction from coming out of a deep sleep. My brain could not process what it was at first. I can't describe it in detail because it only lasted a few seconds. All I remember is it was a very menacing face right in my face.

Our dog was thrown at us, our bedroom light turned on in the middle of the night, and now an evil face wakes me up. This all happened within days of visiting two Oley properties. I was hesitant to go to bed the next few nights due to not knowing what may happen.

Luckily, the rest of the week was quiet, and we figured whatever it was, it made its point and was gone.

Well, that was not the case.

The following Sunday morning, I woke up. The sun was just coming up so it illuminated the room just enough that I could see the entire bedroom. Tami was sound asleep, so I just lay in bed, propped my head up a little with my pillow, and just relaxed. As I did this, something caught my attention out of the corner of my eye. I looked to the right and saw a figure. I just stared in complete amazement at what I was looking at. It didn't walk but glided straight across the bedroom from my right to my left. When it traveled through the space between our bed and the door, I noticed it never touched the floor and hovered about a foot off the ground.

As it moved horizontally along the carpet at the foot of our bed, my eyes stayed locked on it, but it never bothered to look at me. All I could focus on was its static-like appearance. The only way I can describe it is back in the day when a television wasn't receiving a signal, the screen would just show static or what some would call a snowy screen. That is exactly how he looked. I say he because as he traveled across the floor, it appeared to be a male wearing a cloak. He had the hood on over his head, and he was looking slightly down as he made his way out of the bedroom doorway. The first image that came to mind was the Grim Reaper. It honestly was the exact  image minus the sickle.

*Artist rendition of the static figure Jeff witnessed*

Once the staticky figure reached the doorway, I sat up quickly, pulled the covers off, and ran after it.

Tami awakened suddenly and said, "What is going on? What's the matter, Jeff?"

I heard Tami 's concerned voice, but I knew I had to go after what I just witnessed. I ran out of the bedroom and looked around the house, and nothing. No sign of the static guy anywhere. He literally just vanished into thin air.

Totally puzzled, I walked back into the bedroom, replaying in my head what just occurred. Tami was still sitting up in bed with a confused, tired look on her face.

Tami asked, "What are you doing? Why did you run out of here? What the hell is going on?"

I replied, "I woke up and was just laying in bed. Something caught my eye, and when I looked, I saw a figure walk across the room at the foot of the bed and go out the door, so I ran after it."

Skeptical, Tami asked, "You sure you weren't dreaming?"

I said, "I know for a fact I was wide awake. I know what I saw."

Tami questioned, "Who was it?"

I answered, "I have no freaking idea. All I can say is it looked like the Grim Reaper, but all static."

Tami looked at me like I was nuts.

She said, "You're positive you weren't sleeping?"

I insisted, "I one hundred percent know I was not sleeping. What the hell was that?"

This sighting bugged me for days. I thought, *was that the Grim Reaper? Was I going to die? Why did I only see him? Why appear now?*

It sounds silly, but so many questions came to mind.

Two weeks went by without any incident. My wandering mind eased up on the Reaper, and I was less worried it was a sign I was going to die. I figured, if it was a sign of the end coming, it would've happened days later, not weeks later. Again, it sounds silly, but that was my reality at the time.

# Chapter 7

## It Is All in the Static

I WAS CHATTING with Steve on the phone. As we were talking, I mentioned my experience with the static Reaper guy.

Steve said, "Dude! Shut up! Are you kidding me right now?"

I responded, "Huh? What do you mean? No, I'm totally serious."

"Dude, no way," Steve curiously added.

Confused, I asked, "What is going on?"

Steve said, "I saw that same static guy in my house!"

I questioned, "Seriously? When? What happened?"

Steve explained:

> I was laying in bed on my side. The doorway to my bedroom was directly behind me. There is a dresser with a mirror in front of me in the direction I was facing. I opened my eyes, and in the mirror I see a guy standing in the doorway behind me. I rolled over quick, and when I looked at the doorway, he was gone. I turn back to facing the mirror, and this figure is standing in the doorway again. I put my hands under my pillow and close my eyes. Within a few seconds later, I hear what sounded exactly like a shotgun being fired. Dude, it was so loud! It scared the shit out of me! I described him as the static cowboy. He was static like you said you saw. He wore a wide brim hat. He was either a cowboy or Amish. I don't know. He definitely had a hat on. The shotgun going off sounded so real. It freaked me out! My ears even rang. I jumped out of bed and ran downstairs to Lydia.

*Artist rendition of the figure Steve saw in his bedroom.*

I asked her, 'What the hell was that?'

Lydia said, 'What are you talking about?'

I said, 'I heard a shotgun go off! It was so loud!'

Lydia said, 'I don't know what you are talking about. There wasn't any loud noise.'

After Steve described what happened that day, I said, "That is crazy, holy shit! It seems he visited us both. I have to call Shawn and ask him if he experienced anything."

Steve replied, "Yeah, ask him and let me know what he says. Holy shit, dude, this is crazy!"

"I will call him now and get right back to you," I said.

Immediately after hanging up with Steve, I called Shawn and asked, "Hey, I have an odd question to ask you."

"Yeah, sure, what's up?" Shawn responded.

I explained, "After visiting the Oley Farm then going to the cemetery, both Steve and I had a similar entity visiting our homes. We both described it as a static guy."

Stunned, Shawn remarked, "Dude, you are kidding me right now. You are messing with me. Dude, c'mon!"

I said, "No, I am totally serious. This static looking guy visited both our houses."

Shawn uttered, "Hold on."

Shawn yelled to his wife and said, "Crystal! Listen to this! Jeff is on the phone, and that damn thing that we saw in our house was in

Jeff and Steve's houses too!"

Immediately after he finished the last sentence, I heard Crystal scream.

"Shawn! What happened at your house?" I eagerly questioned.

Shawn exclaimed, "That same guy was in our house! I saw him in our kitchen. Crystal saw it too!"

As Shawn described what happened, I could hear Crystal freaking out in the background.

Shawn asked, "Hey, man, can I call you back another time? This is crazy, dude! That thing is in our house! Crystal just saw it! Let me call you back."

I said, "Okay, no problem. I'll talk to you later."

After the call ended, I quickly contacted Steve and informed him that the same figure visited Shawn as well. None of us ever experienced anything like this before. It really made us stop and question what we were getting involved in, and what was this presence trying to tell us? Was he just putting fear in us, or was there another message?

It was unsettling that a similar entity visited all three of our homes.

Even though it was concerning, I did have to laugh because both Steve and Shawn initially kept saying the word dude.

I will never forget that part. First, Steve said "dude" in disbelief, thinking I was messing with him, then Shawn responded the exact same way.

For whatever reason, I do not recall Shawn calling me back or ever hearing exactly what he and his wife saw in their home. Over the years, all three of us would bring it up occasionally in conversation like, "Hey, remember that static guy?"

Shawn never went into detail about it until I began writing this book. Because of that, I reached out to him to see what he remembered and if he could describe when the static guy paid him a visit. We spoke on the phone.

Shawn recounted:

> First thing that happened, I remember standing at my bedroom doorway and looking in at Crystal. As I looked at her, it felt as if someone got real close behind me, leaning over my shoulder. I felt it and then saw a head in the corner of my eye lean in and aside of my head. I turned thinking it was my son messing around. There was nothing there. It was freaky. I swear it felt exactly like someone was behind me and leaning in front. I even saw what I felt was a person's head inches from mine. After I turned and didn't see anything, I yelled, 'What the f@#k!!'

*Artist rendition of the figure leaning over Shawn's shoulder*

Crystal asked, 'What are you doing?'

I said, 'I swore Dylan was behind me messing around.'

Shawn went right into the next story:

> I later walk in the kitchen, and there stands this figure all in black. He wore a wide brim hat. He just stood there staring at me. What's messed up, too, is he didn't have any feet. He was there, then just disappeared.

I commented, "The guy I saw didn't have any feet. He just glided about a foot or so above the floor as he moved across my bedroom and out the door."

Shawn said, "Wow, man! I did not know that. You never told me he didn't have feet when you saw him."

I explained how I found it strange that both Shawn and Steve described him wearing a wide brim hat, and Steve even called him "The Static Cowboy." He wasn't wearing a hat when I saw him, but instead a cloak. It was definitely a cloak with the hood over his head. When he appeared to Steve, he fired a shotgun. Neither Shawn nor I saw a gun. The main consistency throughout each of our experiences is the time frame of his visits. Why would he show himself to me dressed in a cloak, but to Shawn and Steve sporting a wide brim hat? Why fire a shotgun at Steve? Why did he visit us each within a two-week period of leaving the Oley properties, then just vanish, never to be seen again? This experience has always stuck with us. These questions were never answered.

# Chapter 8

## The Review

DURING OUR INVESTIGATION at Shawn's relatives farm, we came away with personal experiences, some EVPs, and the documented spirit energy in the green room.

During the cemetery visit afterwards, we captured a few EVPs. One ominous recording resulted from the moment Steve stomped on Jacob's grave. I had the digital audio recorder on top of the tombstone, and when he stomped on the grave, it came through as a deep, almost hollow thud sounding as if the recorder was located inside the coffin. You would have thought you were hearing a scene from a horror film.

I reviewed the camera footage the next day by connecting the camera to our television and having the audio plugged into our surround sound system. First was the stationary camera we had set up at the top of the stairs on the second floor. I happened to be conducting my review in our living room, and Tami was in the kitchen. The speaker volume was high so I could hear any possible audio captures. When the footage got to the point where Shawn and I went down the stairs to meet everyone outside, a loud whisper came over the surround sound speakers that immediately gave me the chills.

At the same time, Tami hollered from the kitchen, "Woah, what the heck was that?"

As Tami rushed into the living room, towel-drying her hands from washing the dishes, I reached for the remote to replay the footage.

I played it back and we both looked at each other, amazed at what was captured. I replayed the footage over and over again.

To us, we heard, "Gene says, 'Hi.'"

Our daughter, Hannah, was ten years old at the time, and heard it say, "Cheese and nuts." My wife and I laughed so much then and still laugh today over what she thought it said. Audio is subjective, so who knows, maybe Hannah was right, and the spirit was just hungry.

Even though we could not be positive about what the message was, we still stood there in awe of what we heard. These are the kind of moments we look for as investigators. That is why we spend the time and energy extensively reviewing every piece of audio and video footage. It can be a tedious process, but when things like this are captured, it makes time and effort all worthwhile.

I contacted Shawn to see if he knew anyone with the name Gene or Jean that would be relevant to his aunt's house. He didn't know anyone with that name.

Next, I reviewed the handheld video camera that I was holding while we were in the green room.

Steve asked, "Did something happen here?"

Directly after he asked that question, a voice was captured.

We couldn't make out what was said, but it was definitely a male.

During our initial time in the green room, we have Katie's personal experience seeing a figure peek around the corner of the doorway, the anomaly caught on the video camera coming in from the same doorway and entering Lisa's neck, and then I discovered the audio capture after Steve asked if anything happened in that room. Steve 's recorder also captured what sounded like a robotic, computer-generated voice in the attic and drumming in the basement.

I edited all the captured evidence together so we could present it to Shawn 's aunt.

Once finished, Tami, Shawn, and I met Alice and Patty at the farmhouse.

When listening to the audio captures, Alice and Patty agreed to what we thought we heard. As they intently listened, their facial expressions showed both surprise and relief.

We determined some of the audio captures to be unintelligible. While Alice and Patty couldn't understand what was said, they did acknowledge there was something present on the recordings.

They were both glad we captured audio evidence. This definitely helps people have peace of mind with their hauntings. Many don't want to talk to anyone about it out of fear of being called crazy. If you are told enough times that you are crazy, you may start to believe it and second guess your sanity. When we can show someone any kind of evidence, it gives them a sense of relief and validation. Alice believed the drumming heard in the basement was the pipes in the barn. When the animals bump a pipe, the sound travels and can be heard underground in the basement.

We thanked them both again for trusting us in their homes and giving us the opportunity to help.

They expressed their gratitude to us as we packed up our laptop and headed home.

# Chapter 9

## A Second Chance

IBEGAN TO dive into the history of the property. This started with researching who all owned it previously. It can be a tedious part of an investigation. First, I looked at the current owner's deed, which states who sold the property to them. When I learned who that was, I looked at that deed to see who sold the property to that family. I keep doing this until I go back to the original owner. The older the property, potentially the more it switched owners. My research took me back to the 1700s. The farm changed hands numerous times over the years.

Even with the presented evidence, we didn't have any solid answers for why the haunting was happening. Alice's main objective for us to come was to see what we could capture compared to the previous paranormal group that investigated the home. I felt we accomplished what she wanted. Still, I wanted to try and dig deeper into the property by researching and learning everything I could. Naturally, I wanted to go back. I like to return a second time to each location to try and validate what we captured the first visit. Plus, each time we learn a little more about the reasons behind the haunting. That was my intention, but life has a way of interfering with our plans. I became busy with raising kids and other things life threw at me. Even though I was busy, this property always stayed on my mind, and I hoped one day to return.

Within a year of the first investigation, I would get that chance. I received a phone call from Shawn.

He asked, "Hey, I know you talked about going back to my aunt's house in Oley. Well, guess what? The house is now empty, and she said we can investigate again since nobody is living there."

Surprised, I questioned, "Why is it empty? What happened?"

Shawn said, "Woody passed away, so Patty moved back to Ohio. She told my aunt she wasn't going to stay in that house herself."

I felt bad that Woody passed away and felt sorry for Patty losing her boyfriend.

They both seemed to be very nice people. It was a bittersweet moment. I was saddened for the couple, but was delighted by the idea of the house being empty and we would finally have the opportunity to investigate once again.

I said to Shawn, "That sounds great! Do you mind talking to your aunt about setting up a day and time? We will definitely go back."

Shawn answered, "Yeah, sure, no problem at all. I will let you know as soon as I know."

I thanked Shawn, then hung up.

Immediately, in my head, I started going over what I wanted to do during our return to the farmhouse. This news opened so many more possibilities. We would have the entire place to ourselves to investigate how we wanted. An empty haunted farmhouse sounded so cautiously inviting.

# Chapter 10

## The Return

SIX MONTHS AFTER our first visit, we had the opportunity to return to the property. This would give us the chance to gather more evidence in addition to potentially backing up existing evidence. We were excited to return. Tami and I were also joined by Shawn, his brother, Travis, Katie, and our son, Andrew.

Little did we know that this location would find a place to hide and sleep in the shadows of our mind, only to reappear time and time again to make sure we never forget its grip. This moment in time would haunt us for years to come.

It was a cold fall Saturday night when we returned to the farmhouse. What a difference in temperature. The first visit was sweltering, and this time, it was a crisp autumn evening.

Alice came out of her home and greeted us in the stone driveway. She pointed out we could take our time now and have the rental farmhouse as long as we wanted.

Walking in this time, the house had a different feeling. Being empty in addition to the prior evidence we captured, filled the room with the sense of a foreboding.

In the kitchen, we set up a 4'x6' table in the middle of the room with all our equipment and placed the equipment bags on the counters. We brought cameras, digital audio recorders, meters, walkie talkies, and the Radio Shack Hack.

We had enough equipment that took up the entire table we brought. Since we planned on being there for quite a while, we packed our DVR and our IR (Infrared) cameras. Andrew, Shawn, and I ran the cables and set up all our IR cameras and connected them to the DVR. As we did this, Tami viewed the monitor, told us how they looked and if we needed to adjust them. We set up one in the living room, one in the second-floor green room, one in the main bedroom, and one in the attic. Once we had everything connected and ready to go, we each grabbed a walkie talkie, turned off the lights, then split up throughout the four story farmhouse.

*Andrew setting up video camera cables.*

Shawn and Travis went to the attic. Andrew, Katie, and I went to the second floor where the main bedroom is located. Tami stayed in the kitchen by herself to watch the monitor.

Before leaving, I asked Tami, "Are you sure you are good sitting in this kitchen by yourself?"

Tami replied, "Yeah, I'm good. Just go do what you need to do. I'll be fine."

I added, "You have a walkie talkie too, so let me know if you need me."

Most would be apprehensive to sit by themselves in a room known for its paranormal history. Any concerns or fear Tami felt did not stop her from continuing.

I grabbed the K-2 meter, the digital audio recorder, and the Radio Shack Hack, turned, and walked up the stairs to meet up with Andrew and Katie.

Katie, Andrew, and I stood in the middle of what was the main bedroom. I asked Katie to hold the digital audio recorder while I turned on the Shack Hack. As the frequencies scanned, we began to ask questions.

"Is there anyone here with us?" I asked.

Immediately, we heard what sounded like a young girl say, "Hi."

Acknowledging what I heard, I said hi in return. All three of us clearly heard the same thing.

Katie heard a growl.

Concerned, she asked Andrew, "Did your stomach just growl?"

"No," Andrew answered.

Andrew questioned the spirit, "Why did you growl?"

A response was heard, and it sounded like a male voice saying, "Cause."

We replayed the digital audio recorder. Immediately before Andrew asked why the spirit growled, we could hear another voice whisper his exact words, "Why did you growl?"

It was as if whatever was in the room with us knew what Andrew was going to ask before he asked it. It felt to me as if the voice was mocking him. We didn't hear any other responses so the three of us headed down the stairs.

Tami was sitting in front of the monitor watching all the camera feeds as we stepped into the kitchen.

As I flipped the light switch, I asked her, "Did you notice anything on the cameras?"

Squinting, Tami stated, "Nope, nothing yet."

I said, "Listen to this recording we just captured. It sounds like whatever was in the main bedroom with us was mocking Andrew. It was like it knew what he was going to ask before he asked it."

"Yeah, I hear that. That is strange," Tami replied.

Right after Tami spoke, Shawn could be heard talking and walking across the second floor towards the stairs.

Tami stood up quickly, turned off the light, and waited by the stairs.

One thing we do is pick someone to scare, and it's usually Shawn. We jolted his system the first trip to this home, so we figured, why not do it again? All the lights were off as he came walking down the stairs. When he approached the last step and onto the landing, Tami reached out to him in the darkness.

Shawn screamed, "Jesus Christ!"

We could see it all play out looking through the monitor that showed the night vision camera facing the steps. Knowing we got Shawn again; everyone began to roar with laughter.

After we stopped laughing, we all decided to go into the living room.

# Chapter 11

## Let There Be Lights

TAMI PLACED EMF meters on the floor and asked questions to see if any of the meters would spike. She was asking questions and seemed to be getting a response. The K-2 meter was lighting up. There is a row of lights on a K-2 meter that when it senses EMF, lights on the meter illuminate. As the readings get higher, a distinct color will light up.

Tami asked, "Can you make the orange lights light up?"

The orange lights illuminated.

"Can you make the red lights go off?" Tami prompted.

The red lights illuminated.

The meter seemed to go as high as Tami requested. She

called me over to show me what was happening. As I stepped over, I saw the meter stayed in the red, which is the highest reading.

I said, "Step away from the meter so the lights go off, please."

Immediately after asking, the lights turned off. Tami was sitting on the hardwood floor with the meter directly in front of her on the floor. As soon as the lights went out, her head turned to me so fast, and her face was in disbelief. Tami asked more questions, and the lights lit up in response every single time. At one point, she leaned front to move the meter, and as she did, we noticed an anomaly on the screen moving horizontally behind her across the room. The meters kept lighting up to direct questions and would not flicker at all when we were quiet. We tried ruling out natural occurrences that may be making these meters activate. We moved the meters to a different part of the floor and nothing happened. Then we put them back to the prior location, and the lights lit up again. We thought maybe there was an electrical box or wires directly under the floor causing the meters to spike from a power surge or when the furnace turns on. The property owner told us the heat was shut off, so it could not have been that. We continued to discuss reasonings for the spikes, and, just like that, it became quiet.

*Tami watching meters spike.*

I demanded, "If a spirit is in this house, make a noise where you are!"

Seconds later, I noticed the wired tripod camera died. We could still capture audio from the digital audio recorders we had continuously recording in addition to the other wired night vision cameras still connected to the DVR.

"Oh, well, it looks like we are going handheld," I announced.

Once I said that, instantly there was a loud bang on the ceiling directly above us. It sounded like someone wearing boots stomped on the floor. Since the house was totally empty of furniture and had hardwood floors, this sound was very loud!

Katie said, "Did you hear that? It was like a…" Katie paused and didn't finish the sentence. "It was upstairs," she continued.

Travis asked, "Was that upstairs?"

Travis' tone implied he heard it too, but was second guessing his own hearing.

We all did the same as we stood looking at each other in disbelief for a few seconds.

I ran across the living room to go upstairs after the noise.

Andrew was standing at the doorway to the living room.

As he turned and followed me up the stairs, Andrew exclaimed, "That was upstairs!"

We quickly ran up the stairs together to see what caused the bang. As we ran, we heard three more stomps on the floor. Everyone downstairs heard it also.

In a concerned tone, Katie said, "All right, I don't like that."

When we reached the main bedroom, there was nothing there. We walked around and looked in each room. Andrew and I stared at each other in complete amazement. We made our way downstairs. As I followed Andrew down the steps in the dark, I had that feeling of someone or something was with me, walking right behind me with their face inches from my neck. It gave me chills.

As Andrew and I returned to the first floor, Katie, Shawn and Travis were in the kitchen looking at us, waiting to hear what we found. Tami was still in the living room.

I shook my head in disbelief, looked at them and said, "There was nothing there."

Looking up at the ceiling, Andrew questioned, "Can you make that sound again, please?"

I laughed and said, "Oh, that was freaky."

As I looked at Shawn, I noticed his eyes lit up and he anxiously blurted, "Oh God."

"Jeff, this is going crazy in here!" Tami shouted.

I said, "Tell it to stop."

Tami yelled, "Stop it! I command you to stop flickering the lights!"

The lights on the meters immediately stopped.

All of us heard and reacted to that loud stomping sound. Now everyone witnessed the lights going crazy and halting in an instant. I felt everyone was quietly questioning their sanity at that moment. When things like this happen, we as humans use our logical mind to make sense of it, but in the end, after we exhaust all reasoning, we know the only thing left is to label it paranormal. The process usually does not take too long to realize what just transpired was not from our physical world.

# Chapter 12

## Midnight Mouse

I FELT WE should all go to the second floor and see what we could capture or experience. I wanted to just sit, be quiet, and listen.

We stayed together and walked up the stairs to the second floor. I walked in the back room, which was the one that had the curtain in the doorway and where the girls previously experienced the pennies being thrown. Each of us picked separate places in the room to sit down, leaned against a wall, and just listened, shrouded in darkness. After fifteen minutes or so of not hearing anything, I got up and turned the light on. I stood in the middle of the room as everyone else rose to their feet to join me. We were facing each other in the center of the room discussing the stomp on the floor and the meters going off.

Tami said, "It was so random."

She was referring to when the camera died, the stomping, and the meters reacting.

Tami never finished her thought as Andrew spoke up and said, "Yeah, and I was saying to make a noise."

Suddenly, each of our walkie talkies went off and started ringing at the same exact time. It was the sound you send others to alert them. Everybody was startled and took a step back.

Katie screamed.

I asked, "Who made them go off?"

"Who is calling us?" Tami insisted.

Andrew chimed in, "I didn't touch anything."

Shawn added, "I didn't touch shit. It just vibrated in my hand. I swear to you."

"Dude, I want to get out of this room," Katie confessed.

I asked, "They all go off?"

Each person acknowledged their walkie talkie went off.

Tami replied, "That's why I asked, 'Who is calling us?'"

As the night progressed, the energy build-up could be felt, intensifying with each passing hour. The meters, the stomps, now the walkie-talkies.

We decided since midnight was approaching, we would leave and go get something to eat and get coffee so we had caffeine to make it through the night. I kept cameras and sound rolling while we were gone. I grabbed the handheld video camera and set it up on a tripod in the kitchen, pressed record, then exited to meet everyone outside.

We drove to a convenience store a few miles away and were gone for about thirty minutes. The entire time we discussed everything we experienced.

After returning, we all gathered in the kitchen, eating snacks and drinking our coffee. I looked at the handheld video camera and noticed the battery was almost dead.

*Travis, Andrew, and Katie in the kitchen.*

I informed the group, "Guess all we have now are the remaining upstairs IR cameras and the audio recorders. Both handhelds are dead."

We had a digital audio recorder in the living room with us and one upstairs in the back room. We also had the wired camera upstairs

We went back into the living room. Tami and Katie sat on the floor, while the rest of us stood or paced around the room.

Tami and Katie held the EMF meters.

Travis and Shawn continued to ask questions.

Shawn asked, "Are you in here, Woody?"

"Here, we will put all the lights together," Tami said, referring to the lights on the EMF meters.

Travis pointed out, "Look at the three on top."

He was referring to the K-2 meter, which was above the other meters Tami had sitting on the floor. The K-2 was on top, and the other two side by side just below it.

The lights lit up.

"Thank you," Tami responded.

She began reading off the numbers on the Mel meter, "2.2, holding at 2.2. Now 2.0, holding at 2.0. Now 1.9, holding at 1.9. Now 2.0."

Shawn said, "It did that as soon as I asked if it was Woody."

Just as he spoke, Tami read the meter as it spiked to 2.9.

It was so interesting that the meters seemed to spike at this certain area of the living room floor, and especially now that Shawn mentioned Woody's name.

Minutes later, we began to hear a crunching sound coming from the direction of the kitchen.

"What is that? Do you hear that crunching noise?" Tami asked.

Tami got up from the floor and headed for the kitchen. She screamed and immediately hurried back to the living room.

Repulsed, Tami exclaimed, "No way! Hell with that!"

I stood up quickly and asked her, "What's going on? What is it?"

Tami exclaimed, "There is a damn mouse out there on the counter chewing on the tin from your apple pie you bought!"

"Seriously? Show me," I responded.

Tami said, "Umm, no. I'm not going back in there! That is a big nope! I don't like mice!"

I replied, "It's only a mouse. I want to see."

I walked into the kitchen, looked around, and saw the tin on the counter, but no mouse in sight. Then I grabbed the tin off the counter and, sure enough, there were what looked like little bite marks on the one end of it. I walked back to the living room with the tin in hand.

I showed everyone the bite marks. Shawn and his brother didn't seem to mind as much as the girls who seemed genuinely repulsed by it.

Tami said, "If there is one, then more than likely there are more. That is disgusting! Just think, we were sitting on the floor in the dark, and these critters were probably scampering around us on the floor!"

Tami shivered in disgust as she was creeped out by the incident.

# Chapter 13

## A Known Presence

THE NEXT DAY when I reviewed the audio recorders, I was surprised to discover while we left for coffee and snacks, we captured footsteps walking, bangs, doors slamming, and breathing. This happened while all of us were gone. Nobody was in the farmhouse. It seemed someone or something was irritated by us being there.

Also, when reviewing the kitchen video footage, it captured not only the mouse biting the tin, but there were quite a few mice roaming all over the farmhouse. They crawled on the counter and on our equipment on the table. I contacted everyone and told them about the mice and all the noises captured while we were gone. Needless to say, at this point, we were all creeped out by this! Tami was right by saying if there is one, then there has to be more. Crazy thinking as we all sat on the floor in the dark, these mice were quite possibly scurrying near us. Imagine sitting in the dark and feeling something on your leg or arm, turn on your flashlight, and see red beady eyes staring back at you. You jump, look around, and there are mice all over the floor! That is a horror movie all in itself.

One thing for certain, even though some of our audio captured pointed to the mice being the culprit, there was no way the stomp on the floor, or all the slams, bangs, and breathing were caused by the mice while we were gone. There is absolutely no way unless there were some huge critters we did not see.

It was now around 2:00 a.m. We gathered in the living room.

Katie said, "I'm getting cold now. It is cold in here."

I had a sweater on so I took my heavy coat off and gave it to Katie so she could stay warm.

We began to have general conversation as we stood around the room. Katie and Tami sat on the floor even after the mouse encounter, probably because the lights were on.

Travis said, "I'm not trying to sound funny or anything, but when I was standing there," - he pointed to the corner windows- "I don't know if it's the windows going or the wind, but it sounded kind of like a deep voice, ya know?"

*Travis pointing to corner windows*

Tami interrupted, "I thought I heard somebody talking, but thought it was Shawn whispering in his phone."

Katie said, "I know. I heard it."

Shawn countered, "No, my lips weren't moving."

"I heard it too," said Andrew.

I stood there listening to each person confirm what Travis heard. Personally, I did not hear anything. It seemed I was the only one that didn't hear it. After reviewing the audio, a whispering voice was captured, but we could not understand what was said. I was glad Travis spoke up when he heard the voice and happy the others could validate his encounter.

From all our accounts and experiences so far, everything pointed to a male energy occupying this farmhouse. Who is he? What was he trying to tell us? Was he just trying to get our attention? Was he upset we were there?

We wrapped everything up at about 3:00 a.m. Being tired, thinking about the possibility of more mice crawling around with only the floor to sit on and our equipment dying, we ended up leaving.

# Chapter 14

## To Debunk or Not to Debunk

I REALIZED AFTERWARDS, I never looked in the basement for the electric wire that could have caused the meters to go off. It bothered me, so the next day, I contacted Shawn.

I asked him, "Do you mind contacting your aunt and asking her if we could come over to try to debunk what happened last night in the living room with the meters reacting to something? I want to make sure it's not electrical."

Shawn responded, "Yeah, sure. Let me call her and I'll call you right back."

Shortly after, Shawn called me back and stated, "She said it's fine with her, and she would leave the farmhouse unlocked for us if we were coming today."

"Do you have time today to meet me and try and debunk this?" I asked.

Shawn had nothing planned so we decided that noon would work for both of us

.

We met at the farmhouse. The door was unlocked as Alice mentioned. Eager to potentially debunk the meter incident, we split up.

Shawn said, "I'll go in the basement if you want to go to the living room?"

"Yeah, that's fine. Either way is cool," I replied.

As Shawn headed to the basement, I went to the center of the living room floor.

I knocked on the floor so Shawn could find the area while he was down there. I kept knocking until he located the correct spot, and he knocked back.

Shawn yelled, "Dude, there is no electrical wires or box anywhere near this area."

"Stay there. I'm coming down," I hollered back.

As I walked down the stairs to the basement, I hear Shawn saying, "See man, there is nothing even close to that area that would've caused it."

I reached the bottom of the basement stairs and glanced over to where Shawn was pointing.

I agreed and said, "Yeah, absolutely nothing even close. So, what caused it?"

We went back upstairs to the living room and placed the same meters at the exact spots where they originally triggered. Nothing! We tried recreating what happened the night before, and the meters would not even flicker. As we were trying this, Alice came in through the side door, sat in the windowsill, and watched us.

After several minutes with a puzzled look on her face, she inquired, "Can I ask you guys a question?"

I replied, "Sure."

Alice asked, "Can I ask what you are doing and why you are concentrating on that exact spot on the floor?"

I explained what happened the previous night and why we wanted to come back today.

I said, "We don't understand why the meters were spiking and their alarm sounding in this particular spot."

She exclaimed, "Well, I do because that is the exact spot where Woody died!"

Shawn and I both looked at her with wide eyes and the expression of amazement on our faces.

Was that why the meters were going off? I could not say for sure. I knew, but we tried to debunk it, and we couldn't. There was no logical explanation as to why these meters were going crazy the night before.

I thanked Alice for letting us return and told her if anyone that moved into the house experiences activity, we would gladly come back.

# Chapter 15

## Public Notice

FOR YEARS TO come, this home would stick with us. During future investigations at other locations, we would get audio captures of spirit when we would bring up the Oley Turnpike farmhouse.

My intention was to conduct research to try to understand what spirits are at the farmhouse and why they are still there. I was also hoping to get back to the property again. Time flew by with raising kids, working, taking care of our own house, and all the investigations we have conducted since. I would ask Shawn over the years how his aunt was doing. We never had the opportunity to go back.

Seven years later, I walked past a public message board at work. As I passed this board, I glanced over and stopped dead in my tracks. Immediately, I recognized the home that was on a notice for a real estate auction. As I walked closer and focused on the property, I got the chills when I saw it was the Oley Turnpike farmhouse. I thought, *whoever decides to purchase this property has no idea what they are getting into!*

# Chapter 16

## Digging Up the Past

TIME SEEMED TO slip away again. My intention was always to dig deeper to understand why this farm stayed menacing, yet mesmerizing, in our psyche. This puzzle had laid dormant on a table for over ten years. I needed to pick up the scattered pieces that remained and set them in their place.

Both Alice and Randy passed away. I haven't been in contact with their daughter, Lisa, since we first investigated the property. In order to finish this puzzle, I figured she would be the best place to start.

March 10, 2023, I reached out to Lisa via Facebook Messenger.

I wrote, "Hello, I am not sure if I have the correct page. Is this Lisa that lived on Oley Turnpike Road? I was there back in 2010 with your cousin, Shawn. We were there in regard to the haunting."

The next morning at 3:18 a.m., I received a reply, "Yes, it is."

I was glad I reached out to the correct person. I replied to Lisa right after reading her message. I wasn't sure why she was awake at almost 3:30 in the morning, but I figured I'd just explain why I contacted her while I ate my breakfast.

I explained I was in the home in the spring and fall of 2010 due to the haunting and that I had questions regarding that property.

Lisa said she didn't mind, and if she could answer them, she would. She told me that the people who were living in the home at that time are no longer there, and both of her parents have since passed away.

I sent Lisa seven questions I was hoping she could answer. We agreed to meet the following week to discuss the haunting and go over all my questions.

My wife and I met her at an Italian restaurant that Lisa likes in her area. Tami and I arrived and walked in. It has been fourteen years since we saw Lisa. We looked around, but did not see anyone that resembled our memory of her. There didn't seem to be anyone looking for us either. We sat in a booth facing the door and waited. After fifteen minutes, a woman walked in.

I said to my wife, "Is that her?"

Tami responded, "It's hard to tell after all these years."

This woman walked by us and into the adjoining eating area. She began to look around.

As we got up, I said, "That has to be her."

We walked up to her and I asked, "Lisa?"

She said, "Yes, hey, Jeff. I wasn't sure. You both look different. It's been a while."

I replied, "Yeah, we just said the same thing since it's been so long. We weren't sure if it was you."

We sat down in a booth, Tami and I on one side and Lisa on the other. Once we ordered our food, we began to chat.

Lisa began by saying, "I was always afraid in that house."

She was referring to the main house, not the brick house.

Lisa continued:

> It ruined my health. Every time I heard something, I was in the bathroom throwing up. When I got nervous from the house, that nervousness carried on through life at different events. At a birthday party of mine, in the bathroom throwing up. Going to school, I'm outside the bus stop throwing up. Every time my nerves got up, it happened, and it all happened because of that house.
>
> Every time we would do something with that house, paint, new furniture, it was terrible. It was really horrible. I think it was attached to me since I was

born. The red brick house was the original farmhouse. The white house was built after the war. A Medium was at the property one time, and she said she felt there was a soldier there. He was drinking water at a stream. It was there way before my mom's house was built. He had a club leg. He got hurt in the war.

Intrigued, I asked, "What war?"

Lisa said, "I am not sure. I guess the Revolutionary War."

After hearing that, I thought, *that is possible because at the cemetery right down the road from that farmhouse, there are Revolutionary soldiers buried there.*

Lisa proceeded:

Well, we heard that coming up the steps. We would hear a step then a clump, a step and a clump. I wasn't even a teenager at the time. After I heard that, I was in the bathroom throwing up. My mom and I were scared like hell! My dad would go to the mountains to hunt. Every November, he would go up for a week. That's when activity would get real bad. We would be scared out of the house. The windows would shake, screaming could be heard, yelling. We would hear voices say, 'Get out!'

There are people that ran out of the brick house. They wouldn't stay. One guy said, 'You can take that place and shove it up your ass!' (He was speaking of the white house.) That's exactly what one of the guys said. He didn't believe in it. He approached my mom one night at the bowling alley.

He asked her, 'Is it true your house is haunted?'

My mom said, 'Yeah. Do you want to go over tonight?'

There was another woman on the bowling team that was an undertaker's wife. She was just dying to come into this house. She dealt with dead people all the time. My mom told them both to come over that night, and they did.

They came in around 10:30 p.m. My dad didn't like that. He didn't like the publicity, so to speak. People would say, 'You are just crazy,' so he didn't like to deal with that.

There was this one room, which was my brother's room that was always cold. It felt like an air conditioner. It was always cold even though it could be ninety five degrees outside. Well, they go in, and it was totally dark. They had no lights on. They are sitting there close to an hour. The guy says, 'We might as well leave because nothing is happening.'

Lisa paused and said she was getting the chills.

She went on to describe the event:

My mom told me that after he said about leaving, it was instantaneous that this thing appeared on the ceiling. It was about maybe an inch tall. It would run across the ceiling one way then run back the other way. Every time it would run back, it would get bigger. It went from an inch to two inches, then three inches.

They said, 'What in the f@#k is that?'

My mom said, 'Just be still. Be quiet.'

This thing on the ceiling kept growing, and when it got to about a foot in height, these two people that didn't believe in it, got up and said, 'You can take this house and shove it!'

They ran out and said they are never ever coming back in again.

I asked, "What year was this? Late seventies?"

"Yes, it was around that time," Lisa answered.

# Chapter 17

## You Are Asking for Trouble

TAMI STATED TO Lisa, "Jeff is wanting to know the stories to see if what happened in the brick house can in any way be tied to the white house your parents lived in."

I added, "Were any experiences in the main house similar to anything experienced in the brick house?"

Lisa responded, "I personally think it came when I was there because of what I experienced at two years old."

I asked, "What was that you experienced? You believe you almost got killed right?"

Lisa said, "Mhm, and I can see it today."

I had to ask about the age. Lisa recounted a story from

when she was two years old. From my memory, I couldn't tell a vivid, detailed story of that length at two years old.

"So, you can remember this happening at two years old?" I questioned.

Lisa said, "Yes, I can still see it clearly. I was taking a nap."

Lisa didn't finish that particular story.

She paused and said:

> My mom experienced things in the house right away. Others did too when we had picnics. Then there was this Spanish family that got really scared. They were very religious. They had Jesus pictures on the walls, crosses on the walls. I think whatever was in my mom's house moved over to that house.

I said, "You mentioned when you all first moved in the activity was there from day one."

"Yeah, from the first week they were in there," Lisa answered.

I added, "Activity from day one. Then they later used the Ouija board."

Lisa recounted, "Yes, I was two when we moved in. I was about twelve years old when they started using the Ouija board."

I said, "That's what I'm trying to understand. From when you were two years old and felt you almost died until the Ouija board was used, and I was told everything went downhill after that and it got a lot worse."

Lisa agreed:

> Yes. The Psychic went into a trance. My mom said her
> face morphed, and she pointed to my mom and said,
> 'You's are the ones that did this!' My mom wanted to
> get rid of it, but we were told you aren't supposed to
> burn it, but she did get rid of it.

I asked, "Do you have any idea whatever happened to it?

"No. I don't know what happened to it," she replied.

Lisa recounted the story of what happened when she was two
years old:

> My mom was in the kitchen. She heard me screaming,
> 'No, don't do it. Don't do it!'
>
> My mom comes in and says, 'Lisa, what's the matter?'
>
> My mom said that I replied, 'You shut up!'
>
> My mom knew something was wrong. She packed
> my stuff and took me to my grandmother's.
>
> She said, 'Lisa, I want you to tell your grandmother
> what happened in that room.'
>
> I said, 'A man.' There was this man leaning down in
> my mom's bed as I was napping and choking me. He
> had long red bushy hair. He had long fingernails. He
> was dressed in basically a black suit with like a tail
> for in a wedding. He had long hooves on his feet. He
> was trying to kill me. People say at two years old you
> don't talk like that. My mom would disagree. She

would say, 'Yes, Lisa did.'
I think it was the devil. The eyes were terrible. They weren't normal. I believe that was the devil. Then it just escalated. It escalated to the point we were running out of the house! Multiple times. Even in the winter we were running out of the house. It would pick up on certain days. She would have a cross on the wall and it would fly off the wall.

*Artist rendition of the hooved figure Lisa experienced.*

I asked, "Once you moved in and had that experience as a child, who decided it was a good idea to use the Ouija board? Who was in the room? Whose hands were on the planchette?"

Lisa said:

My aunts wanted to ask the Ouija board who was in the house. Well, wrong move. They also had seances. The head person of the seances was the same person that told us we opened the portal. At least four of them were evil. There were good ones, and they were trying to keep the evil ones away from the family. That's why there was so much commotion. It sounded like things were smashing on the floor, but nothing was touched; yelling, 'You get out, you get out,' when there is nobody else in the house.

"Do you remember who all was in the room when they did the board and seances?" I questioned.

Lisa replied:

> My aunt, Tina, my aunt, Bev. My dad was there, but he wasn't in participation. My aunt and I would sit on the deck of the pool and have it on our laps. There wasn't really anything that showed up while playing with it, but just touching it or asking the questions, you are asking for trouble.

I explained that my whole theory on that is that you can open doors. The Ouija board to me is no different than a ghost box or a pendulum. It's a divination tool. Doing things myself, I can open and close stuff. The problem to me is with the Ouija board, you are also dealing with other people's energy. Some things may not get closed or someone participating may have ulterior intent. I feel the more that are involved may cause an unwanted outcome due to the different energies involved. It is all about intention.

Lisa began to tell another story, "My aunt, Tina, lived in the brick house, and she didn't experience anything."

Tami asked, "Was this when they were playing with the Ouija board?"

Lisa answered, "No, she lived there after."

She mentioned a local author that came to the house back in the 1980s, "He brought along four professors from Albright College. They brought that big wheeled tape recorder reel to reel piece of equipment and set it on the stove."

"Yeah, that is definitely 1980s equipment," I responded.

Lisa continued:

> They were asking my mom questions. They went upstairs looking around and they heard a baby cry. One of them said, 'Do you have a baby?' My mom said, 'No, welcome to the party. That is what we experience all the time.'
>
> They went downstairs and listened to the tape, and it was on the tape. They actually heard it. Then this one professor laid flat on the floor. I don't know what he was trying to do. It just seemed like they didn't believe us even though they heard the baby cry. They left, and I don't think they believed.

Side note, I did reach out to Albright College and the local author Lisa spoke of, but I never received any kind of reply.

I said, "When I lived in a haunted house, the activity seemed to be in cycles. It wasn't a constant occurrence. I found the same activity cycles at other haunted homes I investigated."

"Did it happen like that at the farm? Did the activity go in cycles?" I asked.

Lisa replied:

> Sometimes it was every day, sometimes it went in cycles. It depended on the time of year. It depended on if we were having picnics or something. I also believe it fed off of my fear. I remember one Christmas time when I was a toddler. Everybody came down to my mom's house. I was in the kitchen,

and my uncle was in the living room. He was trying to put a little red wagon together. There was a clown doll I wanted that was on the sofa. It was the ugliest clown doll you ever wanted to see. My uncle couldn't get the wagon together and he was getting upset. He let out a couple swear words.

He came out in the kitchen and said, 'Hey, that damn doll in there.'

My mom asked, 'What doll?'

'That clown doll that is sitting on the sofa, does it have batteries in it?' he questioned.

My mom said, 'What are you talking about? It's just a cloth doll.'

He said, 'Well, I'm on the floor in there, I can't get that wagon together, so I'm bitching. I heard something go, ha, ha, ha! It came out of that clown.'

My mom said, 'Well, you know how this house is,'

Lisa began another story that involved her as a child and her aunt:

My aunt and I were upstairs. I was sitting down while she brushed my hair. We were laughing and kidding around. I got a little loud. My aunt says, 'Be quiet. You will wake up your parents.'

She then says, 'Be quiet, Lisa. No, be quiet.'

We both got quiet, and we both heard a step then a clump, step then a clump coming up the stairs. Well, I was ready to throw up.

My aunt said, 'Something is going on. Someone is coming up the steps.'

The next thing we hear is a thud, thud, thud like someone banging on my parents' bedroom door. The door was open a few inches, and when it banged, the door never moved. Well that did it. We were all up. We were all up now. It was horrible. It was just aggravating us.

I commented, "Most people that would move into a place that had activity like you describe would have moved out soon after. Your parents lived there for over fifty years. Why?"

Lisa explained:

We stayed there because my dad was a farmer. He farmed two farms. He would say, 'We aren't leaving this farm. I am a farmer, and that's my job. I have to farm.'

We were tormented in that house for fifty years. My grandfather bought the farm so my dad could farm it. My mom would say, 'Randy, I can't take this. You aren't here all the time to experience it. I am here continuously.'

I questioned, "Do you think the quarry has anything to do with the activity or that stretch of road in general? It's said that limestone plays a role in paranormal activity."

Regarding the limestone, Lisa said, "Yes, it's not just the quarry. The entire village has limestone under it. That stretch of road, there is a ghost man and woman seen too."

"Did activity happen just solely in the house, or did things happen outside too?" I asked.

Lisa replied:

> Things would happen outside too. We would always get together, my aunts, and then at holidays for a picnic. One time, I don't remember which holiday it was, but one time we were cleaning up from a picnic. My one aunt was sweeping up in the kitchen. All of a sudden, she jumps up and over something. The others asked her what the hell she was doing. She explained she saw a black cat with no tail coming towards her, so she jumped over it. Cats would not come in the house no matter how much milk, water, or food was in the doorway to bring it in. The one cat would just growl and hiss and not come in the house. My mom wanted to see why the cat wouldn't come in, so one time she got it to the doorway. When the cat got to the doorway, she pushed it inside with her foot. This cat started banging around to get out. It finally ran out. Two days later, that cat died.

Lisa continued with another encounter:

> It was November. My dad was at the hunting cabin. My one aunt, Toni, and my uncle, Mike, came to stay with my mom. The next morning, my aunt told my mom, 'You won't believe what Mike saw last night.'
>
> My mom said, 'Let's wait until Mike wakes up to tell me.'
>
> Mike wakes up and comes downstairs. My mom asked what he saw last night.

Mike said, 'I will tell you what. I don't know what the hell it was, but I saw it running in the kitchen. It was some black animal with no tail.'

My mom saw the same thing the night before. They both saw the same cat, but only talked about it at that point. The next spring is when my other aunt jumped over it.

I said, "It is so interesting to me you mention a black cat with no tail. When I was investigating a mansion, there was the same thing seen there, a black cat with no tail."

"It's evil. It's demonic," Lisa uttered.

She mentioned that she captured growling on a recorder in the farmhouse back when we were there. I told her that we also captured growling in the main bedroom.

# Chapter 18

## Evil Dwells Here

I ASKED LISA, "Do you remember who all lived in the brick farmhouse?"

Lisa answered:

The people that moved in there before my aunt, Lorraine, and Rich didn't have any kind of activity, but they were the type of people that didn't believe in that. It was the people living in it now, Woody and Patty, the Spanish family before them, my aunt and uncle before them, a man and woman with a boy and a girl prior to my aunt and uncle. That lady had her daughter in the bathtub. She went in to her daughter, and her daughter said, 'Chad and Randy were here.'

There was nobody around. No idea, but that's what she said. My aunt, Tina, was terrified of my mom's house and not the brick house she lived in. The Spanish family after them did experience stuff in the brick house. One time my mom's aunt came to stay with us along with her two sons. She heard about it, but didn't believe in it. There was a blizzard outside, and she left with her two sons. She said, 'I'm never coming back again!'

She didn't even make it one night. When she got to the house, there was no blizzard. My dad's brother had to take her home in the middle of a storm because she was that scared. I don't remember if she heard a voice or heard someone on the stairs, but she was terrified.

Another time when my dad was away at the hunting camp, my mom looked out the window, and there was a guy with an old black suit on and an old-fashioned black hat standing on the porch.

She opened the door and asked, 'May I help you?'

She got the weirdest vibe from this person.

He said, 'Is Mr. Shirey in?'

She told him, 'No, he is farming. May I ask who you are?'

He asked, 'Do you know when he will be back?'

My mom said, 'No, but you can leave a message.'

He said, 'No, I'll come back.'

There was no car in the driveway. My mom said she didn't hear a car come in. She didn't hear a car leave. It was a gravel driveway. You could always hear someone coming in or leaving. My mom thought it was the thing choking me, but in a human form.

Side note, when I was typing this above paragraph and put in the word she, it auto corrected to Gene. I thought, *of all names to appear, it was Gene.* It never happened again during the writing of this story. Coincidence?

Lisa continued, "One time, I can remember something chasing my brother. He was running around the house."

I asked, "What was chasing him?"

Lisa said:

> I think he heard footsteps that came up to him, so he ran. He ran all over the house because it was chasing after him. Going in the kitchen, living room, his room, and kept doing that. He was around twelve or thirteen years old.
>
> Getting back to the Spanish people, my mom said they were a nice family. I think they were in there a week or two, and the guy came over to my mom and said, 'What is wrong with that f@#kin' house over there?'
>
> My mom asked, 'What?' My mom knew about the activity in her house. She knew of some activity when Tina was there, but kind of pushed it off.
>
> The man says, 'I was in the kitchen making dinner at

the stove. I hear this thing running. I turned around, and there was this little dwarf, like a gnome. All of a sudden, it ran.'

They had crosses on the walls, Jesus stuff, and other religious items on mantels and shelves. Crosses would fly off the wall. That would happen at my mom's house too. My mom had one on the table, and it flew off, so you know it was something evil. The Spanish family would keep the lights on in the house all night. They were being tormented by it. I don't remember their names because I wasn't living there at that time.

The time my aunt and I heard the walking up the stairs and the three bangs on the bedroom door, well, we finally went to bed. During the night, my aunt woke up and saw this lady's head at the foot of her bed, and it was glowing.

The lady kept saying, "The bible, the bible, the bible.' She was just mouthing the words.

My aunt didn't want to wake my mom and dad. She was so freaking scared she didn't know what to do. She ended up just laying back down. She just didn't know what to do. The activity would come in droves. Anytime we put up paneling or painted or anything, the activity would intensify. If they rearranged furniture, it would absolutely go crazy. It got to the point, we couldn't sleep at night. It was horrible. It was just horrible.

I asked, "What the guy saw in the kitchen of the red house, did your mom or anyone see that in her house?"

Lisa answered:

> No. The Spanish family saw that often, not only the father. It totally freaked them out. He told my mom more than I can remember. They only lived there a few months. It wasn't long, and they were sleeping in their car in the winter time. One time when we had a picnic, I may have been a teenager, one of my aunt's friends came with her husband. She was pregnant at the time. She went in the house. She was the only one in the house. She went to go to the bathroom, and she heard a baby cry. She ran out of the house screaming. She wouldn't come back after that happened.

I questioned, "Do you feel that after living in that house that it affected your life afterwards in any way?"

Lisa regretfully replied:

> I feel to this day, it was the devil. It affected me in a negative way. I was told we are all born for a reason, but there is a different reason I was born. They say I have a gift to do it, but I'm afraid to.

Lisa was referring to her sixth sense when she mentioned having a gift and being afraid to use that ability.

# Chapter 19

## Parties and Portals

LISA RECOUNTED THE memories of the many parties and get-togethers her family hosted at the farm over the years:

> My mom was a party person. Picnics, parties, whatever. One night, she was having this party. I don't know what let loose, but something in the house, I think they heard a man's voice. I don't remember, but everyone just started running to the door. They kept pulling each other back, it was like "The Three Stooges." Whatever it was, it sent them all into a frenzy. Whatever was there never stopped my mom. She would have birthday parties, Halloween parties, picnics, seances, etc.

Intrigued, I asked, "How many seances do you think

they had there?"

As she took a deep breath, Lisa recalled:

> There was one up in the back attic. I never wanted
> to go up there because there was a cubby hole, and
> there were footprints. Not sure why, but there were
> footprints. It was just horrible. They had a seance up
> there. It was my aunt, my grandmother, a lady named
> Ginnie, and the Psychic.

"Do you remember the name of the Psychic?" I asked.

Lisa said, "I don't remember. It was my aunt's friend. I wasn't
there. My mom didn't want me there. They would bring stuff, and
they would take it up with them."

I asked, "Would they do the Ouija board and seances more than
once?"

"Yeah," Lisa answered, "At first they didn't know it was evil. We
still opened a portal at that time we didn't know exists."

She continued:

> That's when my aunt and uncle were down. My father
> was away at camp. My mom went to get Ginnie, my
> grandmother, and my aunt. As they were coming
> down Oley Turnpike Road, my mom looked, and
> she felt something slip in aside of her.
>
> My mom said, 'Ginnie, wait until we get to the house.
> I'll tell you something.'
>
> They get to the house, and Ginnie says, 'What the

hell was that in the car?'

My mom said a little Indian girl came in the car and was a guardian. She was there to protect my mom. That was the night the horn blew. Ginnie had a horn, and she would put it in the middle of the floor during a seance. I was told she was in the middle of the floor sitting in a chair with everyone else around her. There was a light in the kitchen on. She started chanting. I'm not sure how long time went, but after a while, the horn started blowing. My mom said the horn was so loud you couldn't think straight. Everybody looked at each other like, what is going on? Ginnie just sat in the chair in a trance. My mom said all of a sudden, Ginnie's face transformed into something else. It wasn't her.

That's when she screamed at my mom, 'You! You's are the ones that did this! You's are the ones that opened this up!'

Lisa added:

I feel the health problems I have today are from there. It fermented down in my soul from it. That's why I have the problems today. It's from that house. I remember when we moved there, the people before us, I think the name was Shane, they moved out. The people before them moved out of that house.

At this point, it had been approximately two and a half hours that we were sitting in a booth at this Italian restaurant. I asked all the questions I had and thanked Lisa for her time and telling us all the stories.

I was very appreciative of Lisa taking the time to recount so many experiences from that property, some that made her quite uncomfortable to talk about. When I first met her in 2010, she was very welcoming and open. I left the restaurant that day with the same mindset.

# Chapter 20

## Inn to the Research

I WANTED TO conduct further research. I figured the best place to start would be the community library in Oley. On October 19, 2023, my wife and I headed to the Oley Valley.

We arrived on Main Street and initially drove past the library. We continued further down the street and turned around. As we traveled back, we noticed it was connected to the church.

Years ago, Tami and I had an apartment just a few doors away from the church.

I mentioned to Tami, "I do not remember a library being here when we lived here. That's really odd."

Tami looked at me and said, "Yeah, I don't remember

that either."

We parked in the church parking lot, then walked around front. A little distance past the church was a sign that read, "Oley Valley Community Library."

Tami and I followed the sidewalk to the left. The walkway wrapped around in a curved fashion and ended at what looked to be the basement of the church. The courtyard was very quaint, welcoming, and inviting, something you would expect in this historic village.

Upon entering the library, we were immediately welcomed by a very friendly and pleasant woman by the name of Paula. She treated us as if we were old friends.

After greeting us, Paula asked, "Can I help you with anything?"

I replied, "Yes. I am looking for any information on the history of Oley, but more so a specific property."

Paula informed me, "Well, you are lucky. It's right behind you."

"Perfect," I said as I turned around and we both laughed.

Behind me was a tall bookshelf. It had four shelves each containing various books on the history of Oley. I began to slide each book towards me. One by one, I looked at the titles with the hope I would find what I was looking for. I found four that could possibly contain the answers.

I asked Paula, "Is there an area I can go to sit down and look at these?"

Paula described three different areas where I could sit to look through the books. One was to our right and had more space.

I decided to go to the right and sit in that room. It had a large table and a chair. To the right was a projector on a stand and the screen directly across the room in front of me. On the left side of the room were boxes of crafts for kids.

I sat down and began to look through each book. After about twenty minutes, I felt these books would be a reliable source to find the answers. I didn't want to spend too much time at the library so I figured I would ask about loaning them out.

I went back to the main desk, dropped the four books off aside of Paula, then returned the other books to the shelves where I found them.

I asked Paula, "It's okay if I take these books home, correct?"

"Yes, you sure can," she answered.

"What are your thoughts on the paranormal? Do you want to hear a couple audio captures from my old house," I questioned?

Paula's eyes widened, she nodded her head, and said, "Yes, that would be so cool!"

I got out my phone and played her one audio capture where a young girl's voice can be heard.

After playing it, Paula's eyes grew even wider. She started rubbing her arms because what she just heard gave her the chills.

I played more files, and Paula had the same reaction. She seemed to be creeped out, but fascinated at the same time.

Once I finished sharing the audio clips, I reached over and grabbed the books I was borrowing. As Tami and I left, I thanked Paula for her time and assistance.

After reviewing the books, I returned them one week later.

Once again, Tami and I were greeted by the nice and cheerful Paula as we entered the library.

I handed her the books I borrowed and thanked her for loaning them out to me.

Smiling, Paula said, "Hello there. How are both of you doing? I hope you found them useful. I gotta tell you that after you left last week, I told my husband all about the recordings you played. Those were so cool!"

I replied, "Yes, I did. I am glad we stopped in, and I am glad you liked them."

Next, I asked Paula, "The Oley Inn is open again, correct?"

She answered, "Yep, they are open."

I thanked her again for her assistance. My wife and I said bye and headed for the exit.

As we walked out into the courtyard, I asked Tami, "You want to go to the Inn for lunch?"

She said, "Yeah, sure."

We left our car in the church parking lot and walked to The Inn on Main, which was a short distance from the church.

It was good to see the old building back in business after sitting empty for quite a few years. I love going to all our local taverns, inns, and hotels in the area. There is so much history with each of them. I always feel a connection to these old places.

The host guided us to a back area to a table for four. I was happy because we were away from the main area, so we had privacy, which I like. The only others in this room were behind us a few tables back.

Looking around the room and through the doorway into The Inn, it gave off the colonial feel with the paint color, woodwork, and decorations, all things I enjoy being around.

A young and very nice server introduced herself and took our order.

I said to my wife, "I bet they experience activity here."

"I'm sure they do. It's an old place," Tami replied.

I thought, *just because it's old doesn't mean it's automatically haunted.*

Or does it? I started thinking of all the places we have gone to over the years, and even though the majority are haunted, I don't think it's a guarantee just because the building is hundreds or more years old.

I said to Tami, "I'm going to ask the waitress if she experienced anything here. I feel an older thin male in dark clothes smoking a pipe. He also wore glasses. I'm also picking up on a female energy, but not seeing her."

Tami replied, "Go ahead and ask her when she comes back."

"I will once the people behind us leave. She may not say anything with others around, plus the others may not want to hear about it while they are out for lunch. Many are not believers," I added.

We finished our lunch, which was very good. The server brought our check, but the ones behind us were still seated.

I suggested, "Let's go to the bar, have a drink, and maybe I'll have the chance to ask."

We walked to the front of The Inn and sat down at the bar. Another friendly server greeted us from beyond the bar. We each ordered a drink and relaxed for a bit. After sitting there for a few minutes, our original waitress walked up to the bar beside me.

She jokingly asked, "You guys traded me in for someone else, huh?"

Tami and I laughed. I said, "No, we wanted to check out the bar before we left. That's all."

Now was my chance to ask about any spirit activity.

"Hey, by chance, have you experienced any activity here?" I inquired.

She asked, "Like a ghost?"

I said, "Yeah" and laughed.

"No, but I'm hoping and waiting to," she added.

At the same time, the woman behind the bar turned and looked at us.

I asked her, "Have you experienced anything?"

She said:

No, I haven't. I don't like the basement though. There is this door down there that bothered me at first. One day I opened it and it didn't go anywhere. It hasn't bothered me since, but I still don't like the basement.

I explained, "I am an author and currently writing my third book. It's about a farm on Oley Turnpike Road. I asked about this place too because I love old buildings and believe there is activity here too."

"Oh, that's cool. Which property did you say you are writing about?" she asked.

I explained to her which farm it was.

She said, "Really, that place? I looked into that place for my daughter and I to move in. You saying it's haunted, I'm glad now I never did move there. Wow!"

I thought, *how strange it is that this Inn has been closed for years.*

*It has recently reopened. I investigated the farm years ago. What are the odds that when I recently began writing the story about the farm and stopped at the Oley Library to do research that we would end up having lunch at The Inn, only to find out one of the servers inquired about living in that same house?*

Things like this amaze me. To me, certain events are supposed to happen as they do. Are these events just a random coincidence, or are they guided along by the other side?

# Chapter 21

## Always Believe

I WANT TO take the time to tell the following story. It is another example of the random versus the guided moments in time we all experience.

Days went by, and I said to Tami, "Do you remember the woman's name we spoke to at The Inn on Main?"

Tami answered, "No, sorry, I don't. I'm not sure she said her name though."

I said, "We need to go back. I have to get her name correct and ask her permission to use it in my book."

One weekend night just before Christmas, we decided to head to The Inn on Main. Again, this was a random decision to go on this day and time.

On the way there, I said to Tami, "We have no idea her schedule. We were there for lunch, and now we are going there for supper. I highly doubt she would be working at this time."

"If not, then we will enjoy the good food and drinks and go back another time," Tami added.

Tami and I were greeted by the hostess as we entered. She asked if we had reservations.

Since we do things spur of the moment, Tami said, "No, we don't. Is there room at a pub table or at the bar itself?"

"The only thing available is at the actual bar. Is that okay?" the host inquired.

Tami replied, "Yeah, sure. We aren't picky."

The host said, "Okay, you can go right this way," as she pointed in the direction of the bar.

We could hear the chatter of the patrons as Tami, and I walked in. The place was full. I sat down at the end of the bar and Tami sat to my right. There were only two more seats available at the bar and they were the next two seats to Tami's right. The rest of the seats were taken. This time, there were different servers behind the bar.

I glanced around the room and said, "Well, looks like she isn't here tonight."

We ordered our food and had a drink while we waited. We sat for about fifteen minutes.

Looking around the room, I mentioned to Tami, "I need to get the server's name too from the first time we were here. I was hoping they would both be here, but I don't see either."

As I turned my head back towards the bar, I noticed out the corner of my eye someone pulling the chair out aside of Tami to sit down. I turned my head to the right and looked over the back of Tami's shoulders and saw the person I was hoping to see so I could get her name. There was a little girl with her. The child sat aside Tami, and the woman sat next to her in the only seat left.

I nudged Tami and whispered, "I think that's her."

Tami looked at me. I lifted my chin as if to point to the woman that just sat aside her. Tami turned, looked at her then back at me.

"Yep, that's her," Tami said laughing.

I immediately thought, *what are the odds we randomly pick a night to return to The Inn, the time we go, it's full, and the only seats available are at the bar, then after we sit, there are only two more seats left, nobody sits in them until a woman and a child sit in them, and this woman just so happens to be the one I'm looking for?*

Tami turned and said, "Hello. We talked to you before. My husband is writing that book."

She replied, "Yes, hi. I thought you two looked familiar."

I said to her, "The last time we were here, we talked about that farm on Oley Turnpike Road."

The woman nodded and said, "Yes"

"I am currently writing and would like to put that conversation in the book. Is that okay with you?" I added.

Again, she nodded and said, "Yeah, that's fine. Sure."

Tami asked, "Can he use your name?"

She agreed.

Tami asked, "May I have your name?"

She responded, "My name is Kourtney, and this is my daughter, Harper."

Tami and I both said hello to Harper.

I texted Tami their names so I had them for the book and so we would know their names in case we would run into them at the Inn on Main.

I thanked Kourtney for letting me use her name.

Tami started chatting with Harper about her fingernail polish.

I said to Tami, "I will be right back."

I went to the car and retrieved my two other books I wrote and took them inside The Inn to give to Kourtney and Harper as a gift.

Kourtney thanked me and asked if I would sign them.

Harper asked, "What kind of book is it?"

"They are about ghosts," Tami replied.

I added, "You might want to get permission from her mom before you talk about ghosts with her."

"Oh, no. It's okay. We watch those shows," Kourtney replied.

I signed both books and handed them to Kourtney.

Harper opened the book I signed for her. Her mom read what I wrote.
Harper,
Always believe.

Harper added, "In ghosts."

We laughed at what she said. I wrote, "Always believe," to mean for her to believe in herself, in Angels, in the other side, and, yes, Harper, you are right, and in ghosts.

We thanked Kourtney again and told Harper that it was nice to meet her.

Tami and I left and noticed a crowd of people on Main Street. We walked over and there were hundreds of people gathered on the street facing a band that was on the porch of The Inn. They were all there to sing Christmas carols and wait for Santa Claus to arrive. It was an amazing sight to see. At that moment, it really felt like Christmas. Looking at all the people that gathered on the street together, the band on the porch, the flags waving, and the old historic homes that were slightly illuminated by the streetlights made it feel like we were back in time. It's something you don't see too often nowadays. Technology seemed to take away these types of gatherings. My hats off to all the ones responsible for the event and for all that gathered.

It was a very special moment in time.

We left with an all-around great experience inside The Inn on Main and also outside afterwards.

# Chapter 22

## Another Point of View

AFTER LEAVING THE farm, my plan was to conduct research and try to answer all the questions that arose from both our investigations of the brick farmhouse. Days turned into months then faded into years. During the writing of this book, I really wanted to sit down and talk to anyone that may have had experiences at the Oley Farm and were willing to tell me their stories. I reached out to Shawn and his two brothers, Chris, and Travis. They each helped the best they could, but they weren't sure who would be willing to talk about it. They reached out to different family members, but it seemed nobody wanted to talk about the subject. I felt it was never going to happen. Then one day, Chris told me his cousin, Renee, and her mom, Tina, may want to discuss that farm. They lived in the brick house for years and spent time at that farm so they may have stories to share. Chris said I should try and reach out to Renee.

I looked her up on Facebook and sent her a message. Renee replied and said she would ask her mom and get back to me. Days passed and I thought, *well, I tried. Guess this may never happen.* Then I noticed a message alert pop up, and it was Renee saying her mom would sit down and talk to me. I was elated to hear that. Finally, I got to sit down with more individuals that were part of this property. We decided to meet at her aunt Bev's, which is her mom's sister's and also Lisa's aunt. Tami and I knew Bev because we investigated her home a few years after the Oley Farm, but have since lost her contact information. Shawn and his brothers didn't know how to contact her either.

The evening of Friday, February 2, 2024, my wife and I arrived at Bev's home. As we pulled in, Bev opened her front door to let us know she was home, and we could come in. She held open the door as Tami and I approached the porch. We walked through the door and into the living room. Bev sat down on her loveseat. Tami sat aside of her as I placed my equipment bag on the floor and sat down on the sofa that was straight across from them.

I said to Bev, "It's been a long time since we saw you. We came here twelve years ago due to the activity you were experiencing here. How have you been? Do you still experience things?"

Bev replied, "I've been okay, and, yeah, I still experience things."

I asked, "If I remember correctly, you and someone else saw a figure, some kind of mass go through here in the living room and go down the hallway?"

Bev answered:

Yeah, that was my brother-in-law that was here with

me that saw it too. It went through here in the living room and went all the way down the hall to the back bedroom. I got up and went after it, but it just seemed to disappear.

The door opened and a woman came in. I said, "Hello, how are you?"

"Good," she said as she sat beside me on the sofa, "I'm Lea, Bev's daughter."

"Hello, nice to meet you," I replied.

A few minutes later, the door opened again and in came who I figured was Renee and her mother, Tina. Tami came over and sat between Lea and I so Tina could sit with Bev on the loveseat. Renee grabbed a chair from the dining room and sat down.

I said, "The reason we are here is because of the book I am writing about our experiences at the Oley farmhouse in 2010. We went in the brick farmhouse."

Renee asked, "Did anything happen there?"

I explained:

> Yeah. Our meters went off while we were there. We left at about 11:30 p.m. to go for coffee. I had audio recording the entire time we were gone. When we listened to the recording, you could hear what sounded like doors banging, slamming, breathing.

Tina exclaimed, "Oh my God! Never. Never heard anything there. Ever."

"Was there an Asian lady living there?" Tina asked.

"No, it was a woman named Patty and her boyfriend, Woody," I answered.

Then I mentioned how at one point during our investigation, my wife was sitting on the floor in the living room while Shawn was asking questions pertaining to Woody and all of a sudden, it sounded like someone was in the room directly above us stomping on the floor really loud. I told them my son and I ran up the stairs after it to see what it was because it was really loud due to the house being empty.

Tina asked, "Where were you at?"

I replied, "The living room, and above I believe that was the main bedroom. Patty told us she would wake up with a figure standing beside her bed."

Tina uttered, "Oh my God!"

I said, "She was kind of heavy set and what scared her was whatever energy was there, knocked her off her feet as she walked through the kitchen towards the side door. It just laid her out."

Surprised, Tina questioned, "Really?"

Renee admitted, "The only thing I was ever afraid of there was the attic door when you sat in the bathroom on the toilet."

Lea agreed, "Oh, yeah" as she nodded her head.

Tina said, "I was never afraid there. Never ever. I loved that house. I didn't even want to move. I think maybe there were bad and good ones in that house. That's what I think."

Bev chimed in, "The ones in Alice's house were evil."

Tina nodded her head and said, "Yeah"

Tami asked, "You said after you left there someone else moved in. You said it was a Korean couple?"

"Yeah, it was a Korean lady. It was only her though," Tina answered.

I mentioned, "When we first went there, Alice said she had trouble keeping people in there. The one family left in the middle of the night during the winter and slept in their car."

Everyone nodded their heads and said yeah in agreement.

Lea said, "Yes, they were tormented a lot."

Tina commented, "The Asian woman put her bed on the side porch."

Lea added, "Yeah, she refused to sleep in the house. They loved Tina because whoever was there didn't want her to leave. Everything after that, after she left, was bad."

I asked Tina, "Did you have experiences there? Did you ever notice anything?"

Tina replied, "No. I used to be down in the cellar alone, cutting wood, and doing my crafts. I'd be down there for a couple of hours."

Bev looked at Tina and asked, "What about the time I was there on the weekend?"

Tina said:

> The only time was one night when she would come over on the weekends after her husband passed away. She slept in the room where the bathroom is, the one back there. We heard all kinds of noises up there. I had never heard it before. I never heard it before and never heard it again.

I asked Tina, "Did you ever experience anything in Alice's house?"

She responded, "I'd never go in there by myself. Say we were having a picnic or something, I would never go in that house alone."

I turned the discussion back to the brick house.

I mentioned, "When you go up the stairs, there was a room to the right. We called it the green room. Patty had that padlocked shut."

Shocked, Tina said, "Oh my God! Really?"

"Yeah, she had it locked, and she had a line of salt across the floor at the attic threshold and the green room threshold," I added.

Tina said:

> The only thing in the attic, even in the winter there were all kinds of bees and flies. I'd have to go up there and clean them up every month or every other month. I can tell you that all the years there, the closet

across from the bathroom door, I never opened it.

My intention was to ask why they thought Alice's house was negative and what might have caused it to become that way. I remembered Alice telling me about the Ouija board being used there. I needed to look into it further, so I asked her sisters.

I stated, "I remember when we first went to the farmhouse, Alice was telling us about the activity in the main house, and she didn't want us going in there. She talked to us about her playing with the Ouija board."

Tina replied, "Yeah, we did that. We went down there. Everyone went down there every weekend and did all kinds of stuff."

"Yeah, but that was after you guys were hearing stuff," Lea added.

All agreed as they nodded their heads.

Tina said, "Yeah, and then it got worse."

Lea chimed in, "I even asked the others, and they never believed in any ghosts until my Aunt Alice's house."

"It started out with us all going down and playing cards. Then it turned into all that," Tina added.

Tina looked at Bev and asked, "Who was doing it (meaning the Ouija board) when they told you about Teddy and all?"

Bev replied, "Teddy and I were trying to do it. It wouldn't work when I did it. It was him and Karen. It would not do anything when I tried it."

"Whose board was it? Was it Alice's?" I asked.

Each person chimed in, and the census seemed the owner of the board was either Lisa or Alice.

Tina whispered, "It's creepy."

I asked, "Is that why you all did it, just wanted to see what would happen due to all the activity there? You wanted to connect to it?"

"We wanted to do it. We had fun every weekend," Tina answered.

Lea said laughing, "You can't count how many times we ran out of there."

Tina and Bev said the kids would be under the table.

Bev added, "Lea was always the first one under the table. The rest followed."

Lea remarked, "They knew something was going to happen because I would be under the table first. Then all us kids would be under the table. We would hear things or something would happen."

Tina stated:

> There is something else I want to tell you too. I was half asleep in my house now. It was a few months after we moved. All of a sudden, 'Tiiinnnaaa' filled the whole room. (Tina said her name but drawn out.) It filled my whole bedroom. I don't know what that was. Also, the summer after we moved, I went over to Alice's to go swimming. I got over there and went in the pool a little bit, then I got out and I hear,

'Tiinnaa.' I thought, well, I think I'm going home.

I asked, "Was it a guy's voice?"

"I don't know what kind of voice it was. Then when I went over again, I heard the same thing calling my name," Tina replied.

Lea said, "Yeah, the outside of that house was just as creepy."

"That is one of my questions. Being in that house, leaving, and moving to different places, do you think anything from the Oley house followed any of you?" I asked.

Renee confessed, "I was worried about coming here because I don't want any of that in my life or in my perfect little house. I was like, are you sure we aren't going to bring any of it to Bev's house?"

Lea added, "It's already here," creating an ominous feeling in the room.

"I don't want to open any doors like they did with the Ouija board," Renee replied.

Lea remarked, "There is already stuff in this house."

Bev chimed in with, "Yeah, and I'm not afraid of it."

Lea pointed at her mom and said, "She isn't afraid of it. She looks for it. It's not like when we would run each other over trying to leave the house. She runs after it."

"I don't remember anything from the Oley house," Renee added.

Renee looked at her mom and questioned, "Did you tell them the story about me coming down the steps?"

Tina began to tell us the story:

> I was making a pot of coffee in the morning. Renee came down the steps. She started screaming, 'Mom! Mom! A lady is trying to choke you!'
>
> I turned around and was like, 'What?'
>
> Renee yells, 'There is a lady trying to choke you!'

Renee added:

> I vaguely remember the whole story. My memory is so bad. I don't know what's going on with my memory. Either Lea has to remember something from then like a cousin thing or my friend, Shannon, would remember our growing up stuff, hanging out because I got nothing.

Tina said:

> I hear more things happen at my current house. I was in the basement doing my laundry. I hear this pounding on my back door. It was just pounding on the door, no knocks before. I go up and there is nothing there.

# Chapter 23

## Terrifying Tales

TINA CONTINUED ABOUT the Oley house.

She said, "At the other house, my husband would hear noises. He would ask me, 'Were you upstairs?'"

"He would never elaborate though. Tina would say, 'No,' then he would just let it go." Lea added.

Tina agreed.

Tami mentioned to everyone that we see a phantom cat in our house.

Renee said:

That was another thing at Alice's house. There

were always cats at the farm, but they were never ever allowed in the house. Never do I remember ever seeing one in the house, but they would always see cats, and they were always tailless. There were always tailless cats. They would come in and go under the table. Then they would look and nothing there.

"That is crazy!" I remarked.

Renee asked, "Why did you take one home with you?"

Everyone laughed.

I explained:

I have a book out called *The Minersville Mansion*. There was a black cat there that had no tail. People saw it, and now you are telling me about a cat with no tail. We see a cat like that in our house, but it looks to have a tail.

Renee stated, "It was at Alice's house all the time, not in the brick house, but in the white house."

Discussing all the activity, it appeared to unlock a hidden corner of Renee's mind. She began to tell us other memories of Alice's house.

"All I remember is the silly things you all used to do. We would all go sit in the one room everyone thought was scary," Renee stated.

As soon as she said that everyone chimed in at the same time, "Chad 's room!"

Renee continued:

> We would just sit in there in the dark and wait. We
> would see lights bopping around on the ceiling then
> go up into the corner and then go into the other
> corner, then everyone would run completely out of
> the house. That's the actual memory I have.

"Yeah, and Alice would just knock you over," Tina added.

Bev questioned:

> Remember that night they were doing the Ouija
> board? They were all around the table. Then all of a
> sudden, there was something in the living room. You
> could see this, and everyone took off. I was the only
> one there. Karen was trying to go out the door. She
> would open the door, and I would push it shut. She
> would open it, and I would push it shut. There was a
> highway right there, so I'd get scared when everyone
> would run. So finally, they all ran upstairs into Alice's
> bedroom.

Lea exclaimed, "Yeah, which would be the last place I'd run!"

Bev continued, "They all ran upstairs. I stayed downstairs. I
was standing by the door. I saw this thing forming. Someone asked,
'Where's Bev?' I yelled, 'I'm coming!' I jumped in bed with Randy!"

Tami asked, "Did it look like it was going into a human shape?"

"Yeah," Bev replied.

I asked, "You guys experienced this, but you kept playing with the Ouija board after that?"

"Yeah, we did it every weekend," Tina answered.

I had to laugh at how she said that statement so nonchalantly.

Tina said, "I never did it."

"Me either. It would never work for me," Bev added.

Both were referring to the Ouija board.

Tina shared another experience with us:

> The one guy that used to come down, Rich, well, he left. It was around two or three in the morning. He was driving on Memorial Highway. He said he was driving and, all of a sudden, he went through a big tractor trailer. You know what he did? He went and beat on a minister's door to baptize him. He kept knocking until he answered.

Totally intrigued, I asked, "Really?"

"Yep, it's what he did," Tina stated.

Renee added, "It was like a ghost truck."

Bev pointed to Tina and said, "I saw my husband in her house."

Tina agreed, "Yeah, I saw him too at the other house."

Bev said:

> We were painting. I could feel someone behind me.
> I turn around and I say, 'Hey, what are you doing?'
> He stood there leaning. He just stood there like he
> always did when I was doing something. He stands
> there and grins.

Tina added, "Yeah, I saw him at my house outside the door like he was trying to find the key or something."

Renee asked the others, "Didn't Alice's toilet flush on its own?"

"Always," Lea chimed in.

Bev said, "Mine here does too. The water turns on too. It would just blast away."

Lea mentioned, "There were numerous times at Alice's house we would be sitting around the table and, all of a sudden, the toilet would flush. We would all just look at each other like, did that just happen?"

I asked, "So, do you all think even though the activity was there when Alice first moved in, it got worse once everyone messed with the Ouija board?"

Tina said immediately, "Oh yeah!"

Bev followed with "Yeah, it was terrible!"

Renee added, "I remember you all saying it was because of us kids and all our energy. As we got older, it seemed to calm down."

Bev said, "Yes, I think it's because of being teenagers. I believe that's true, especially the teenage years. You are going through a change."

I asked, "Do you feel it was evil before the Ouija board? Do you think that had anything to do with it? Was it nasty prior?"

Bev answered, "Yes, remember the one thing that was choking Lisa?"

She continued:

> One night, I am down there, and Alice said, 'Chad is sleeping in his crib, so will you stay here and watch him?' I said, 'Yeah, I guess.' I hear this click, click, click, click. It sounded like a light switch. I hear it again. Click, click, click. I snuck in and Chad was sleeping. I went out and thought, *Chad, you are on your own.*

Tami asked, "What made you guys run out? Did you see something or hear something, or was it the inner fear of just being in the house?"

"No, we were just scared," Tina replied.

Bev added, "Yeah, it was just the fear of being in that house. I never ran."

Lea stated, "We always heard something."

"Like voices, or what was it?" Tami asked.

Lea said:

> We would hear voices. I know when I was a teenager,
> we would go up into the attic. Of course, we were
> kids, and they had all kinds of old stuff up there.
> There was this cubby hole. As scared as we were,
> we still wanted to see this cubby hole. So when we
> got near, and being scared already, we would hear a
> sound, a movement, could have been a mouse. There
> was always something. Some kind of noise would
> scare us.

Lea described an experience she had while she was in the basement:

> The one time I was sleeping overnight, and they didn't
> have a shower upstairs, only one in the basement. We
> had to shower in the basement. There was one vent
> in the living room floor that you could see down
> because that's where the heater was. I remember
> I was down there taking a shower and I started
> screaming because I thought Chad, my cousin, was
> peeking down at me in the shower. I yelled, 'Alice get
> in here! Chad is peeking down!' Chad wasn't there.
> He was outside. I know I saw someone looking down
> the vent at me.

*Artist rendition of the figure Lea saw looking down the floor vent.*

Lea intrigued us with another story:

> One time, there was a bunch of people there. I went to the kitchen door. Somebody knocked on the door. I moved the curtain first to see before I opened the door. There was this shadowy thing, so I never opened the door. I didn't want to let it in! It freaked me out, and I was like, 'Nah ah." I looked again, and there was nothing there.

I stated, "I remember Shawn saying something about the attic and the cubby hole being creepy."

"Yeah," Lea agreed.

"Yeah, that was scary," Renee added.

I asked, "Have any of you noticed anything outside on the property that was scary? Like in the barn or anywhere?"

Tina answered, "The animals would carry on something terrible."

Bev added:

> Yeah, one day Teddy was sitting in the chair by the window at the porch in the front. We heard all this pounding and banging. The windows were rattling. So we all got up and we ran outside and there were all these birds flying out of the trees and the animals were running all over the place.

Tina stated, "You know when Alice got sick, she said, 'When you go to Florida, will you take these two little ones along? They never get anywhere.'"

"We were going to Florida. I never asked her who they were. She saw two little ones," Tina added.

Bev mentioned, "In the hospital, Alice said, 'All these people come at night, and they keep me awake talking. Freaking people talk all night.'"

"One night she said they were having a party," Tina added.

Renee remarked, "Well, I think at the end, they all start coming to you."

I replied, "Yes, I agree with that one hundred percent."

There are multiple accounts of people who were very sick or close to death having phenomena referred to as end-of-life experience or deathbed visions. Alice was known to be sensitive to the energies of the spirit world, so was that the reason so many were coming to her? In my second book, *The Spirits of Shoemakersville Road,* I describe how one time Mary Lou was sick, and she seemed to respond to others in the hospital room that her family could not see.

Tina interjected, "Alice even looked at her daughter-in-law and told her, 'You are pregnant.' Here to find out then she was.

"Somebody must have told Alice, whispered in her ear," Renee added.

Tina agreed.

"Yeah, and I don't want to hear that. I don't want to ever hear that again," Bev said in an uneasy tone.

Lea stated, "Well, that happened down at Alice's house, so tell him."

Bev said:

> It was Christmas. I found the picture of Chad sitting in the chair right where you come in the door to the kitchen. I went over and sat on the sofa beside Alice. I just started crying. They were like, 'What's wrong, what's wrong?' I said, 'Something is talking in my ear. It's talking in my ear.' It was hard to understand, but I knew what it was six months later. In six months, I cried.

"My dad passed away then," Lea added.

Bev said, "I knew something was going to happen, and I knew it was going to be him."

I asked, "With all the things that happened there, do you think it was something different each time, or was it the same energies each time?"

Tina replied, "No, they were different."

Bev agreed, "Yeah, they were different."

"That makes total sense," I said.

Renee stated, "Alice, her whole life she smelled dirt. She would put Vicks under her nose because she would smell dirt. Then when her son, Chad, died, she stopped smelling dirt."

"Yeah, I said to Alice afterwards, 'You don't use Vicks anymore,'"

Tina added.

I asked, "So she smelled it her whole life, then it stopped after he passed?"

Tina replied, "I think it started when she was pregnant."

I questioned, "Was the accident he had at the intersection of Route 662 and Turnpike Road? I know there were a lot of accidents at that intersection."

"No, but that one young girl was killed there," Renee answered.

Tina said, "Yeah, and that one family."

Renee added, "Yeah, they pulled out in front of a truck, and they were in a van, I think."

"That is what I am trying to figure out. Was the activity due to the Ouija board? Was it there before? Was it from the accidents? Was it everything together that caused so much to happen at this property?" I questioned.

Lea said, "We were there every weekend. I was scared to hell. I can tell you I never got up to go to the bathroom myself in that house."

Renee began to tell a story:

> I remember one thing that did happen to me that I
> remember when we lived at that house. It happened
> in the main bedroom. I thought it was possible
> because I partied back then that maybe it was from

that. I remember coming out of my bedroom, walking past my mom's bedroom and looking in. It was like this wicked...

Renee paused for a moment, then continued:

Well, there were two other people. I know it wasn't my mom and Donnie. These people looked like they were moving my mom and Donnie. It looked like they were having this wicked, ugly sex. It looked out at me in the hallway, and I just remember running into the bathroom because I was getting up to go to the bathroom. It was weird. It was really weird.

Tina remarked, "Creepy. Really creepy."

I asked, "Have you all believed in this stuff your whole life, even before Oley?"

Tina replied:

Yeah, when I was little, my aunt lived in a really haunted house. It was on Locust Street in Reading. I slept over there. I couldn't fall asleep. I turned around, and there was a closet there with a curtain. There stood a man with a black cloak, a flashlight, and a little doggie. They had to take me home. That house was haunted.

Bev's description of the cloaked man definitely aligns with the figure that I saw glide across my bedroom after our first investigation.

Lea stated, "My mom's aunt had psychic abilities like my mom. She would actually tell Alice things too."

Tina added, "That was a bad house. That house was haunted. It would knock her down her steps. This thing would come down the steps as they were going up and knock them down the steps."

"Has anyone ever gone to the farmhouse and not experienced anything?" I asked.

Lea answered, "I haven't met anybody that has gone to that house and didn't have some sort of experience."

Bev said, "Even people that didn't believe and said we were nuts came and they ended up running out. They never came back to the house."

Tina added, "Ya know, one night, I got a phone call in my sleep. It was a horrible voice. It was like you heard down at Alice's," as she looked at Bev.

"It was freaky. I have no idea what it said. It was just mumbo jumbo. It was in my dream I answered the phone, and it was that weird voice."

Bev stated:

> People think I'm nuts, but when my husband died, I was living for a year and a half by myself in East Reading. I went to bed. I just laid down and this banging started on the headboard, just banging like a kid kicking his feet. It was a...

> Bev paused, unsure if she wanted to continue. She scanned the room, then decided to finish.

"It was a leprechaun," she said.

I am still scared. Just look at me. I told it to stop, and it just looked at me. I said, 'Get out!' He said, 'No!' He just kept kicking in the top of the headboard. Then I screamed at it to get out!

Tina added, "I would have ran!"

I asked Bev, "Is that the only time you saw it? Anytime in later years?"

Bev replied, "No."

"I will never live alone. I am not being alone!" Tina muttered.

I asked Bev and Tina, "Have you had experiences growing up at all, or was it just when you got older?"

Tina replied, "No, we never even thought about that stuff."

# Chapter 24

## The Connection

IFOUND IT fascinating that Tina remembered a story, but nobody seemed to have had many paranormal experiences prior to the Oley Farm. This really intrigued me. By their accounts, it looked like Bev, Alice, Tina, and their aunt all had some level of supernatural ability. I believe what they all said, so why would their abilities only seem to manifest once Alice moved to the farmhouse? Did they become more aware as a result of them opening doors to that world by the use of the Ouija board and the other ways of divination they described? Also, why was Tina so fearful of it all?

Renee stated, "It wasn't until Alice moved down to that farm. We all lived in the city, so it was a big deal to go to the farm. Felt like we drove an hour. We would sleep over, but would only sleep in the living room."

Lea added:

> Like Renee said, we would never sleep anywhere else but the living room floor. All us kids would stay together on the floor. We would never sleep anywhere else. It was a small house so you didn't have to go far to go to the bathroom. If you had to go to the bathroom, you didn't go. You would wait 'til morning until daylight because it was that scary.

Renee agreed and said, "It was terrifying! It was terrifying!"

I asked, "Have you ever seen a static type person?"

Each of them shook their heads and answered, "No."

"I only saw it forming," Bev added.

I went on to explain the static figure that Shawn, Steve, and myself experienced.

Renee knew about the cemetery I spoke of and the farmhouse that sat on that property.

Renee said, "That farm had a fire, and part of it burned."

I replied, "Yeah, it happened a lot over the years where places that are haunted start on fire."

"The shed did at Alice's house," Lea added.

I stated, "It happens quite often."

I asked, "With all the things that happened at the Oley farmhouse and with everything experienced after, does anyone feel the activity after is connected to that Oley house?"

Bev replied, "I don't know. I don't know."

Renee and Lea both said they never felt it was related.

Lea added:

> I only ever experienced two things in my current home. It was right after our cousin, Chad, got killed in the car accident. I saw my cousin, Chad, in his red hat go from my one son's bedroom into my other son's bedroom. I only saw him one other time. I never experienced anything else, so I don't know.

I stated:

> One of the reasons I am asking is to see if you all feel it was connected to that house or if you feel it's just certain people are more open to it, and it doesn't matter where you go, you will experience something?

Lea replied, "I think with my mom especially, she is more open to it. She does have a little bit of that gift. My dad would always tell my mom, 'I don't want to hear it. Don't even say it.'"

Renee added:

> I feel if it was coming from the Oley house, we would all be having other experiences. Once we weren't there anymore, once I left from being kids, I never had any other kind of ghost experiences. Supposedly

the guy that lives currently in Alice's house doesn't notice anything, but his wife does.

Bev said:

When I moved in this house, I usually have that feeling. When I moved in here, I didn't. It was only when I lived here a little while. The bedroom I only slept in for maybe five days. It's a brand new bed. I probably may have slept in it three times an entire night. I don't go back there.

I mentioned:

I find it interesting. I ask similar questions wherever we go regarding things that may have followed from a previous home. A few of you experienced things after the Oley house. I wanted to ask to see what you all felt about it.

Tina stated, "They say when you go to yard sales and drag stuff home, it could have…" She didn't finish her sentence.

I knew where she was going with this, so I nodded my head and said, "Yes."

Immediately Tina said, "I'm getting rid of everything."

Everyone burst out laughing.

"Tomorrow everything will be outside in a pile," Renee added.

Tami said, "Yeah, on a pile that says, 'May be haunted.'"

Renee said, "Take at your own risk."

We all continued to laugh.

I was really enjoying hanging out with them all. I got a kick out of Tina. The way she would just nonchalantly say things, I couldn't help but laugh.

I stated:

> Energy is attached to everything. When you buy things at an antique store or secondhand place, energy can be attached to an object. When I go to a home with activity and they say they lived there for years and nothing happened until recently, the first thing I ask is, 'What changed?' Something had to have changed. One question I ask is, 'Did you bring something home from a second hand or antique store, a yard sale?'

> We cleanse everything we bring home because energy is attached to things. Over the years, people have gone to those types of places, brought things home without cleansing them, and they began to experience activity from the objects they brought into the house.

Renee asked, "Well, what about me? Almost everything in my house came from a flea market, and I don't have anything. I would buy the oldest, craziest stuff, and I have never experienced anything."

Tami said, "Maybe you just got lucky."

I added, "I feel a lot, if not all the places like antique places, would tell you that they experience some type of activity."

Tina responded, "I never experienced anything in my home until I brought things like that home. I never did."

Bev shared her experience about when she sensed things with a jeep.

As she looked at Lea, Bev asked, "Remember that jeep? There were two of them there."

"Yes," Lea answered.

Bev explained, "She was looking at two jeeps. The one I touched, I said, 'Don't get it. Lea, there is something wrong with this car. Don't get it. Do not get that car. Something is going to happen to it.'"

Lea added, "Three months later, it caught on fire. Yep, she knew."

Bev said, "We were on vacation. We were in the car. It began to smell so bad. I started to get a headache."

"We didn't smell anything," Lea stated.

Bev continued:

> Something is wrong with this car. We made it down there to where we were going, but then a couple blocks down the road, it died. Another time we were going somewhere, and I said to Lea, 'I shouldn't be going. Something is going to happen. Something is going to happen, and I don't want to go.' I ended up going anyway, and that's when Nicky died.

I asked Bev, "Are you open to the fact you are open? Do you realize you have abilities?"

Bev replied:

> Yeah, I've always been like that. I had dreams of falling when we were kids. I didn't know if it was me or someone else falling. Here it was Shawn's dad, Brad. When he was a kid, he was trying to jump and fell down the stairs. I saw that in my dreams. Things even happen now. I go places and things fall off the shelves by themselves. Happens all the time.

It was interesting she mentioned that because it happens to me as well.

I didn't want to take more of everyone's time. I greatly appreciated the time they set aside already for me. I was ready to say thank you, but Tina said she had one more story to tell me.

Tina said, "Alice asked me to come down to the farm. I got down there and was going to stay overnight. Renee was very little. I think she was a baby."

Renee added, "I'm sure this story ends with, 'I was too scared, and I asked for them to take me home.'"

Everybody broke out in a roar of laughter!

Tina continued her story:

> Anyway, Alice and I were watching television. Alice said, 'I'm going to bed.' I said, 'Okay,' then I got scared. Alice came out again, and all of a sudden, it

was like the whole house started rattling. Alice and I curled up with Renee. It stopped, and Alice went back to bed. I figured, well, guess I'm going to go to bed too. I went in, but got up and called my brother at two o'clock in the morning to come and pick me up.

Renee said, "Told ya!"

We all roared with laughter again.

I mentioned, "If anyone thinks of anything else and you want to tell me, please reach out. I'll be happy to hear it."

I thanked them all and told them I appreciated their stories, their time, and it was nice to meet everyone. Tami and I grabbed our coats and headed home.

Months later, Bev had a story to tell me that took place back in the 1970s when her father-in-law was boarding a flight to Poland. She took her in-laws to the airport. Bev watched as they walked down the aisle to board their flight. Her father-in-law turned and came back to her. He looked at her and said, "Goodbye, Betta," a name he always called her. Once more, he looked at her and said, "Goodbye, Betta." As he turned and walked to board his flight, Bev got a weird feeling and believed she would never see him again. She mentioned that the Ouija board never worked for her, so her cousin and husband asked the board if Bev's father-in-law was coming back from Poland. The board answered, no. Next, the planchette began to spell out, "Telegram will come."

Within a week, they received a telegram that was written in Polish. Once translated, they discovered her father-in-law died.

# Chapter 25

## Current Residents

ON FEBRUARY 10, 2024, Tami and I were in Oley to eat lunch at one of our favorite places, The Inn on Main. It has been fourteen years since my last visit to the farm. I always wondered if the current residents were experiencing the same activity in each house as others did before, would it be something new, or would they say they aren't experiencing anything?

As we ate our lunch, I asked Tami, "What do you think about stopping over at the farm to see if anyone is willing to talk to us?"

Tami answered, "We can if you want."

Even though she agreed to stop by, I knew she was hesitant to return due to the experiences we had there and afterwards. I fully understood why, but my curiosity got the best of me, and I had to find out.

I decided to let the powers that be make the call. I said to Tami, "When we drive by and nobody is outside, then we keep driving. If anyone is outside, then we pull in and see if they will talk."

Tami nodded her head and said, "Okay."

We finished our lunch and headed to the farm. As we were driving, I knew Tami was thinking, hopefully, nobody is outside so we can keep going.

At the same time, I thought, *please be outside, I need to find out.*

As we approached, we both looked to the right, scanning the property. I didn't see anyone, and I was ready to say, guess it wasn't meant to be.

Suddenly, Tami pointed and said, "I just saw two people in the backyard of the smaller house."

I did not notice them, and Tami could have easily said she didn't see anyone so she could avoid stepping back onto this property, but I was glad she did.

We drove down Oley Turnpike Road, turned around, and returned to where Tami saw them in the yard. We pulled in the lane that separates both farmhouses. I felt reluctant, but at the same time eager to be back.

A man and a woman stood in the backyard of the smaller house. They were moving about, but stopped immediately and stood side by side watching us slowly drive in and down the lane. We stopped, got out of the car, and approached them.

Upon greeting the couple, we learned their names were Carl and Cindy Forster. I said that I had a few questions for them. I mentioned visiting the farm in 2010 when a woman named Alice lived here and the family had a lot of things happen on this property, and it had been many years since we visited, so I wanted to stop to see if you were experiencing anything regarding the paranormal.

They both shook their heads and said, "No."

I explained I wrote a few books on my paranormal experiences over the years and my next book is about this property. Also, I informed them that I wouldn't be doing my due diligence if I didn't stop in and question the ones that live there currently to see if they personally experienced or heard about any paranormal activity at the farm.

Cindy answered, "We heard things, yeah, about it, but, um, we lived here four years, and only thing is every now and then we find things missing. We never see anything, but things disappear, and at times, we find them somewhere else."

She looked at Carl and asked, "We don't see anything have we?"

He shook his head and said, "I haven't, no. Actually, I don't believe in that stuff."

Cindy shared:

> I do. I had many experiences. The locks to lock
> and unlock the door. It's weird because one time I

could go out, I lock it with one key, and then have to unlock it with another key, not the one that goes to it. I could never figure out why it's the other key sometimes. Sometimes it's the right key, sometimes it's the other key. It's really weird. Other than that, no. Like I said, we lived here for four years. We heard from somebody that knew back then that a little boy drowned in a pool.

Tami and I had never heard of anyone drowning in a pool. We remembered Alice having a pool, but never that happening in the fifty years they lived here. As often happens, tales are told about haunted properties that are embellished to make the place sound more interesting. This place didn't need that. It had so much activity, additional stories weren't necessary.

I said, "I will ask about that, but we have no knowledge of that happening."

Carl mentioned that he knew the place was built in the 1800s because he believes the name of the guy that built it and the year can be seen when the sun shines directly on the barn.

I told them that this was one of my questions during research, and I wondered if there was another house here prior to the current ones.

I knew that the homes here are dated early 1900s. If the barn shows the 1800s, then I would have to look into that name and time period.

Carl pointed to the brick farmhouse and stated, "That guy has been living in that house for fourteen or fifteen years now."

Surprised, I replied, "Wow, really? That would mean he moved in there right after we investigated it when Patty moved out."

I knew it was important that I spoke to this gentleman.

I explained to the couple about the deed research I conducted regarding the property.

Cindy added, "I heard there was a family that lived here for a little bit, then they left. They left because things were happening."

She was speaking of the Spanish family. This was an accurate story told to her compared to the fabrication of the little boy drowning. I always find it interesting how we perceive what we do and why.

Tami pointed out, "Jeff, the guy is outside over there if you want to talk to him."

Carl added, "See, now, up in the attic in the window over there is Jesus hanging on the wall. I don't know if something happened up there or not."

Cindy said:

> I would never sleep upstairs. It's a big attic. It's spooky. There are no lights in there. It is, it's spooky. I would never sleep upstairs. Never. There are two bedrooms down and the one upstairs. There could be two upstairs, but, no, it's too spooky.

She continued, but changed the subject and began talking about the haunting, "See, I thought it became that because of the little boy that died in the pool. That's when I thought it was haunted."

She described how the cellar felt freaky and can't bring herself to go down there at night or early in the morning. One time she heard something and thought somebody was down there, so she took one of the kitchen chairs and placed it under the doorknob because she was the only one home.

"I would have done the same thing," Tami replied.

Carl asked, "What kind of activity did they have here?"

I explained several things regarding the use of the Ouija board, seances, and other activities that took place.

Carl looked at her and said kiddingly, "Maybe we should get a Ouija board and see what happens."

Cindy demanded, "No, we are not getting a Ouija board. No, no, no."

We all laughed at her response.

After hearing a few stories, she replied, "I never saw anything like that. If we did, I don't know we'd be living here."

She looked over at the brick house and said, "I can see it at that house. Sometimes that house looks creepy."

We were there for about twenty minutes. I didn't want to inconvenience them, so I thanked them for their time, and Tami and I headed back to our car. I wanted to talk to the ones living in the brick house, but I figured it would be better to stop back another time.

One thing I noticed while I spoke to the couple was how the property changed since last being there. Looking around, the barn and outbuildings seemed more worn and weathered than I remember. Honestly, I had an uneasy feeling about it. It felt as if someone was watching, hidden and they couldn't leave.

Was it from the past, or was I sensing something currently about the place? I knew for sure, though, that this property would be a perfect location to shoot a paranormal or horror film. It just had that look and energy about it.

I now put all my focus on researching and finding out what was on this property prior to the current homes since the barn is dated back to the 1800s.

I also find it very interesting that the previous family lived there for fifty years, experiencing paranormal activity the entire time and sometimes very frightening incidents. This couple lived in the home for four years and have not experienced anything close to it. The question that may come to mind is, how is that possible? Is it due to the former owners opening doors to the paranormal, which came with consequences solely to them in that house, and now that they are gone, so are the spirits/entities? Was it just a connection to that particular family? Carl isn't a believer, but Cindy is. Must one believe and be open to it in order to experience some level of activity, or are the non-believers just labeling them with natural explanations rather than the supernatural? These were several questions that arose in my thoughts as we drove home.

# Chapter 26

## Bringing It All Together

I HEARD THE terrifying accounts of family and friends who had lived or visited this Oley Farm, but I still needed to find out what caused the activity to happen in the first place and continue for fifty years. A number of scenarios crossed my mind that made sense to me, but my need for documented proof still weighed on my mind. I tried reaching out to various sources in and around Oley, which included the library, historical organizations, court records, the local inn, the current residents of the white farmhouse, and all the research sites I have on the internet. My next step was to contact the residents of the brick farmhouse and to conduct further research. Tami wrote a letter that basically stated why we were in the home years ago and if the current resident had any experiences to please reach out to us. We drove to the Oley farmhouse and placed the letter in their mailbox. We figured that would be the best way to contact them instead of knocking on the door. We found that in more recent years, residents of homes do not acknowledge when we knock on their doors. Years ago, that wasn't the case. People's perceptions over the years have changed. Most people today just do not want to be bothered.

Weeks passed, and we did not hear anything back from them.

Tami wrote another general letter in which she asked the other residents along Oley Turnpike Road if they knew any of the history of the Shirey Farm property including any paranormal activity that took place over the last fifty years. We drove to Oley again and placed the letters in the mailboxes of all the neighboring properties along that stretch of road. As we drove, we noticed a hemp farm called Oley Health & Wellness was open, so we stopped in. Jeffrey Brooks, the owner, was very pleasant and welcoming. He couldn't give us any information on the old Shirey property, so he referred us to another farm. He told us this farm has been around a very long time and they would possibly know more. We bought a few products from Jeffrey and drove a mile or so to the farm he suggested.

We arrived and bought produce at this farm. The first farm was very welcoming, but that feeling became the total opposite while we visited this next farm. We left there a bit disappointed in the reaction we received. After a week of not getting any responses to our letters, I went back to the various research accounts that I have online.

I kept going back to the stories that I was told. It didn't seem like others believed their prior or later experiences were connected in any way to what they went through at the Oley Farm. A handful of similarities made me question that.

Tina spoke of a man she saw while she was sleeping over at her aunt's when she was a child. She described a man standing in the closet wearing a black cloak. I experienced a man wearing a black cloak in my bedroom after visiting the farm for the first time. Alice told of a man wearing a black suit and hat that knocked on the door asking for Randy. He seemed to just appear and disappear. Lea saw a black shadowy figure on the porch when she looked through the curtain. Lisa even recalled the bushy red-haired guy with hooves as wearing a black suit. Could this all be the same man?

Steve and Shawn both encountered a man in black wearing a black hat. This happened in the same time frame I saw the cloaked man. Was this the same entity and only appeared slightly different to each of us? He fired a gun when Steve saw him, but just stood in Shawn's kitchen staring at him. If it is the same man Tina saw when she was little, he had a flashlight and a little dog with him. Was this the widely recognized malevolent entity, The Hat Man? This supernatural figure has been seen wearing a hat and at times a cloak. Could it be The Hat Man, or was it someone that lived on the farm and has since passed?

One family, who lived in the brick house after Tina, was tormented by what the father described as a dwarf or a gnome. Bev called what she saw in her home as a leprechaun. Is this the same being?

There are many supernatural beings that are believed to exist depending on one's heritage. Some may appear small to one person, but human size to another and even have the ability to shapeshift.

Beings that may be mistaken for a leprechaun are: Puca, Fairies, Changelings, Djinn, Goblins, Brownies.

Since this area was settled by German immigrants, I wanted to look at the beings in German folklore: Kobolds, Erdgeist,

Heinzelmännchen, Wichtel, Zwerge, Erlking.

If we go back further, the Native Americans believed in: Nature Spirits, Pukwudgies, Skinwalkers, Nanabozho.

Were some of the beings that made themselves known to the family and friends at the Shirey Farm part of the land for centuries and only presented themselves once the house was built? If that is the case, then most, if not all, the owners of the property would have similar stories.

Did they only come through once the family began using the Ouija board and after conducting seances? Was it an open invitation without them realizing it?

Since Tina and others have stories of activity prior to Oley, could some of these entities be connected to the family and later followed them to the Oley property and to their current homes? Is there a connection?

All these scenarios played over and over in my head. Would I truly find these answers, or would I settle for what I perceive to be true and hope you reading this will agree?

I decided to go revisit the deeds I researched to see if I could connect one of the previous owners to the man in black. This was the same figure who once visited Alice looking for Randy, and who was later seen by Shawn, Steve, and me in each of our homes after the initial investigation. My research took me back to 1757 when a man named Frederick Hill purchased the land and paid for it in pounds. That date would make sense since the Native Americans left the area around the French and Indian War, which began in 1754. During the deed search, one man stood out as the possible figure I could tie to the man in black. His name was Lawrence Mathias. He held a few positions in the community, but two stuck out to me, one being the Justice of the Peace, and second, the Sexton for the Salem Reformed Church. Would he have been known for dressing in black and carrying a gun under one or both positions? I spent hours trying to locate a photograph of this man, but no luck. Tami and I decided to drive to the church and take a chance if someone was there. No luck at that either. After we came home, I went onto the church's website. I emailed them in hopes they would have a photograph of him in their records. I received no response from the church.

There were multiple owners of the property. Many of them may have dressed in black. People dressed differently back in those days. Today, there are so many photographs of people due to the convenience of smartphones always at their fingertips, but that wasn't the case years ago. I spent numerous hours on the research alone, but I kept hitting the same roadblock. Research is not as easy as they make it look on television. These shows sit down with a local historian, and they produce photographs, documents, illnesses, and other pertinent information of a specific person. I have never found research to be that readily available, revealing, or simple.

The one entity that has stood out to me over all the years was what has come to be known as The Hat Man. Who was this man? Was he once an owner of the land? Had he formed some sort of attachment to this family prior to moving to the farm? Did he come through the door they opened from playing with the Ouija board, or did they conjure him up from the seances they conducted? Could he have been Jacob from the cemetery? It has been written that Jacob died under mysterious circumstances. Since The Hat Man didn't do any physical harm to anyone, was he merely a protector from all the other supernatural happenings on the farm?

I wanted to reach out to a good friend of mine, Dana, and see what she felt by looking at the two photographs I took at the cemetery back in 2009. I sent both to her without telling her the location or why I had the photographs. I just asked if she would look at them, particularly the figure standing at the wall in the one and afterwards tell me what comes to her. Within five minutes, I received a reply text.

Dana responded, "It looks like a shadow figure, but my gut says man with a hat."

To say I was blown away by that reply is an understatement. Of all things to say, she mentions a man with a hat. What are the chances? I explained to Dana why I sent the photographs and what happened in our homes in the weeks following our investigation.

Dana replied, "So Steve disrespected his grave, so that makes sense. That's just what my gut says, and the man may have also died of a gunshot as well. If you can remember the grave, someone should put flowers on it."

I have wanted to do the same since that night in 2009. Dana suggesting it now made me want to make sure it happened. Even if The Hat Man wasn't Jacob or anyone from the Schneider Farm, it is a possibility since the Schneiders at one time owned five hundred acres of land. Did that land once adjoin the Shirey Farm property, or was it part of it at any time? My records show that at the time of the Cox trial, Hannah Hill and Jacob Spang owned what later became the Shirey Farm. Trying to connect any of the previous owners of the property to The Hat Man was a daunting, if not impossible task. What I could do is go back to the cemetery with Steve fourteen years after our last visit.

On August 27, 2024, Tami and I drove to Oley to visit the Hetrick Farm, the same farm that was once the Schneider Farm where Susanna Cox's tragic story took place. I wanted to ask permission to go back to the cemetery once again.

As Tami and I exited our car, Charles Hetrick came out onto the porch. I explained who I was and the times I visited over the last thirty years. The family was always friendly to us when we asked before, and this time Charles was just as welcoming. He gave us permission to walk back to the cemetery while we were there and with Steve at a later date.

About three or four years after investigating this farm, I experienced a traumatic event that turned my life upside down. This event opened me up to the spirit world and made me look at life in literally a whole new light. During this journey, I thought about tuning into the Oley farmhouse to see what messages I may receive. I wanted the answers, but I was always hesitant to use my abilities to focus on this place that had so many negative stories attached to it. The battle in my mind was between, is it really negative there, or is it just perceived to be? Did I really want to focus my energy on it? What may be the consequences of doing so? Everything has a cause and effect. For me, it can be physically and mentally draining focusing on the energy of another person or place. At times, it affects me in such a way, which can and does take its toll. I always want to stay in the light and not give any attention to the dark or something of ill intent.

August 28, 2024, I decided on a resolution: to confront this figure directly. I focused on the farmhouses with the intent of finding out who this figure was and what it wanted.

Home alone, I closed my eyes, relaxed completely, and focused on my breath. In that state of calm, I journeyed to a place beyond our physical world- a place I call home.

I asked, "Who are you? What is your intent?"

I heard a male voice respond, "C'mon, Jeff," followed by a chuckle.

When I heard c'mon, it was pronounced as c'moin. "C'moin, Jeff." This was slightly unsettling at first, but I felt that the way it was spoken meant that I knew who it was, so why am I asking?

I asked again, "Who are you?"

The same voice answered, "I'm going to show your team in about forty-five minutes."

That statement confused me. I write as I hear things. It definitely sounded just as I wrote it down. What did that mean? Show my team what? Who was my team?

Next, I heard, "I saw him, but I looked away from him."

As so often happens, I hear things that could be past, present, or future. At times I hear dialogue or bits of a conversation that took place or will take place at the location I am connecting to. I honestly never know. All I can do is try and interpret it and hopefully fit that piece of the puzzle in its place.

Once more I asked, "Who are you?"

A different male voice responded, "It's bigger than us." The tone was calm and peaceful. I found this to be a profound statement, which made me stop and think, suggesting that some things are beyond our understanding and comprehension on the physical plane. Over the years, I knew this to be true, but I was just reminded by the spirit world.

# Chapter 27

## A Final Resting Place

SEPTEMBER 8, 2024, was the day Steve told me he would be available to return to the cemetery at the Hetrick Farm. We arrived at approximately 11:00 a.m. As we walked the path leading to the graveyard, we discussed how it has changed since we were together at this property. I pointed out all the high Johnson grass that Tami and I saw just weeks prior. The only difference was that the high grass was pressed down leading up to Jacob's tombstone. Both Tami and I do not remember ever walking close to it due to the possibility of ticks. Whatever the reason, it was good to see we had a clear path this day.

Steve and I stood facing Jacob's tombstone.

Steve said:

> Jacob, I come bringing these flowers as a gift and an apology for what I did fourteen years ago. I didn't know back then what I was doing. I apologize for it. I am hoping this will be closure for all of us.

Steve knelt and placed the flowers on the ground in front of the tombstone.

*The flowers Steve placed at the tombstone.*

As he did, he added, "This is from me. I apologize for what I did, so please take this as a peace offering."

Steve wanted to read a prayer of forgiveness that he felt was fitting for what we were doing there today.

Steve read:

> Lord help us to extend mercy to others and forget the past so that we can move forward toward our futures. Forgiving Father, please forgive us for not being forgiving. Forgive us for holding grudges, thinking evil thoughts, and seeking revenge. Forgive us for hatred and malice.

I appreciated Steve for doing this. We did what we felt was the right thing to do and that was to try and bring closure by returning to the cemetery.

After placing the offering at the tombstone and reading the prayer, we paused for a few seconds then walked out of the graveyard. We can only hope the spirit heard Steve's plea for forgiveness. But in the world of the unseen, such answers are not always immediate. It had been fourteen years since we first disturbed the spirit, and only now after all this time did we offer what was long overdue. We left uncertain if this gesture would bring peace or if it had come far too late to lull what was awakened.

In the beginning, I wrote about how multiple people sharing the same moment can remember it in entirely different ways. I ran into Renee recently and she told me a story, which I heard at one point over the years, but for some reason, it slipped from my mind. How can a memory lie hidden in the corners of our mind, but then summoned from the shadows once the words are spoken again? Strange, yet fascinating workings of the mind.

Renee described an encounter when she was nine years old sleeping in Chad's bedroom. She told me she woke up to the sounds of the pinball machine that was in his room. She looked and saw the red-haired hooved figure standing there playing the pinball machine. She was understandably terrified, so she slowly pulled the covers up and over her head. When she later looked again, he was gone. Why did this figure appear to both Lisa and Renee? Lisa believed this being wanted to kill her, but during Renee's encounter, the figure was playing a game. Either way, this was yet another example of the countless stories told to me from the ones tormented on this farm. It is what nightmares are made of.

A few days after speaking with Renee, I contacted Lisa. During our conversation, she recalled a memory from childhood when she had been sleeping with her mom, and Chad slept with his dad. Chad woke up in the middle of the night and saw spirit lights all over the bed. At that time, I also questioned Lisa about who brought the Ouija board and whatever became of it. Initially when I asked, Lisa couldn't remember. I figured I would ask again. She informed me that she believes her dad buried it on the farm. Hearing this, an unsettling tension began to build. I got an image in my head of someone one day digging. They hit something solid, reach down and pull out this square weathered and worn object. They blow off the dirt and a deep instinctive fear washes over them that this is something that should never have been unearthed. Was that part of the reason I felt like something was hidden, watching when I visited the property recently?

I have always tried my best to answer the questions I pose, but in the end, not all the answers came. Some things, I guess, we are not meant to know. They are out there, waiting to be revealed when the time is right. I can say, yes, this is definitely what happened and why it happened, but at the end of the day, I only know what I perceive to be true. I find myself no closer to the answers I sought. I have pieced together what I could, drawn conclusions from what I've seen and felt, but even now, the truth remains hidden, constantly seeming to slip just out of my reach. Is that the nature of this place, or is it the nature of all things unknown? Maybe the past held the answers. Maybe the spirits were tied to this place in ways we will never understand. Whatever the truth is, it belongs to everyone who sets foot on the property. It is theirs to experience, theirs to question, and theirs to carry with them, as it has always been with me. Perception is a fascinating subject to me. Our reality is shaped by how we see it, and each of us sees it differently. Everything is open to interpretation. What I know for sure is that this place holds more than meets the eye. What it reveals depends on who is looking.

Dana summed up my thoughts perfectly during our last discussion on the Oley farm when she stated:

I believe every individual has different energy to offer and some are compatible with the beings/spirits/energy of the home or land, like it is the perfect food for it. It's active when it's fed and dormant when starved. I would bet it is currently sleeping. It is not gone.

Someone else will wake it up...

*Be careful what doors you open,
You may not like what is on the
other side.*

# Acknowledgments

Thank you to:

Alice and Randy Shirey for allowing us into your home. May you both be at peace.

Lisa Shirey- Seyfert for joining us on the initial investigation and for speaking openly about your supernatural experiences.

Bev, Tina, Lea , Renee for sharing your paranormal encounters. I truly appreciate your willingness to talk about them and trusting me with your stories. Also thank you Bev for welcoming us into your home once again.

Shawn Shaffer for your  thirty years of friendship foremost.  If it wasn't for you, I would not have this story to tell. Thank you for joining us on the investigations and for your patience with all my never ending questions.

My wife, Tami, for being by my side no matter what life brings. Thank you for all your hard work designing this book cover. It turned out perfect.

My three kids, Andrew, Hannah, and Lauren. My success in life will never be titles or achievements, it will always be the three of you.

Nadine Witmer for being such a close friend, your editing skills, and for just being there for me in general.

Katie Fetzer for your passion for the paranormal and for being a special part of our family since you were a child.

Steve Reber for being a good friend and for you and Lydia joining us on our first investigation at the farm. We shall never forget the static man.

Travis Shaffer for joining us on our second investigation at the farm. What a great time that night was. Also thank you for your friendship and your help as I wrote this book.

Chris Shaffer for your friendship, time, and patience answering all my texts and your help while I wrote this book.

Bianca Giannantonio for your amazing talent in bringing to life what was described by those who experienced the paranormal events at the farm. The way you sketched them is nothing short of incredible.

Dana Vollmer for being a friend and always for your openness to work as a team to understand the messages from spirit. Many times we are on the same frequency.

Kourtney for always being so welcoming and friendly when we visit The Inn on Main. Also to your daughter Harper. Remember to always believe.

The staff at The Inn on Main for the great service, food and conversation.

The Schwenkfelder Library and Heritage Center, The Oley Valley Community Library, The Berks County Recorder of Deeds office, and Berks County Association for Graveyard Preservation, for your time and assistance as I conducted research.

# Sources

The Oley Valley
A Photographic Journey
By Oley Valley Heritage Center

Oley Valley Heritage
The Colonial Years 1700-1775
By Philip Pendleton

Pennsylvania Dutch
Folk Spirituality
By Richard E. Went

The Passing Scene
By George Meiser, IX
Gloria Meiser

# Citations

Masson, Joel. The hat man ominous silhouette of a man wearing a top hat in the room. Paranormal sleep paralysis shadow man ghost figure. Adobe Stock. https://stock.adobe.com/images/the-hat-man-ominous-silhouette-of-a-man-wearing-a-top-hat-in-the-room-paranormal-sleep-paralysis-shadow-man-ghost-figure/778944508?prev_url=detail

Cam, AR. Black cat head on black background. Adobe Stock. https://stock.adobe.com/images/black-cat-head-on-black-background/508617596?prev_url=detail

Rodriguez, Fran. Ouija board in a table with candles. Concept of spiritism on Halloween. Adobe Stock. https://stock.adobe.com/images/ouija-board-on-a-table-with-candles-concept-of-spiritism-on-hallowen/461294676?prev_url=detail

See the haunting come to life.

Scan the QR code to see the evidence of the property featured in the book.

Thank you for your support!

# Bio

Jeffrey A. Dengler is a husband and father foremost. Family is everything. Jeffrey's journey into the paranormal began many years ago. The catalyst for his involvement started when he was in his early twenties living in a haunted home. Later in life, Jeffrey experienced a traumatic event that opened him up even more to the spirit world. This event was truly humbling for him, and it affected him to his core. It was all part of his awakening. Jeffrey has a passion to help others by utilizing his knowledge of the paranormal field and what he perceives are his God given abilities which he believes everyone possesses. He feels it is divine guidance and a push to be there for others in this way.

www.ingramcontent.com/pod-product-compliance
Lightning Source LLC
Chambersburg PA
CBHW061442150726
47987CB00001B/312